Do-It-Yourself

...udio

MUSIC THEORY

BY TOM FLEMING

PLAYBACK+
Speed • Pitch • Balance • Loop

To access audio visit:
www.halleonard.com/mylibrary

Enter Code
6877-6038-0124-8471

ISBN 978-1-70510-272-5

Copyright © 2022 by HAL LEONARD LLC
International Copyright Secured All Rights Reserved

Visit Hal Leonard Online at
www.halleonard.com

Contact us:
Hal Leonard
7777 West Bluemound Road
Milwaukee, WI 53213
Email: info@halleonard.com

In Europe, contact:
Hal Leonard Europe Limited
42 Wigmore Street
Marylebone, London, W1U 2RN
Email: info@halleonardeurope.com

In Australia, contact:
Hal Leonard Australia Pty. Ltd.
4 Lentara Court
Cheltenham, Victoria, 3192 Australia
Email: info@halleonard.com.au

CONTENTS

INTRODUCTION

Why study music theory? The simple answer is that, as in so many areas of life, knowledge is power. Some understanding of the inner workings of a given musical situation can unlock possibilities that are simply not available if you are just playing the notes that happen to be in front of you. If you have any desire to compose, arrange, or improvise original music, you will benefit hugely from this study, which helps explain not only what is going on but why; without it, you will be essentially stumbling around in the dark.

Traditionally, musicians have often studied only the areas of theory thought to apply to their instrument or style; classical musicians will know all about the writing of music and technical terms that enable them to sight-read almost anything in any key. Rock and pop musicians tend to have a deeper understanding of chords and harmony, allowing them to improvise appropriate accompaniments and solo ideas with ease. This book aims to bridge this divide and assist musicians in all styles to understand the fundamentals in a broader sense and in doing so, perhaps help dissolve some of the barriers between these different types of musicians.

About the Audio

The price of this book includes access to audio online, for download or streaming. Using PLAYBACK+, you can adjust tempos and set loop points, among other features, allowing you great flexibility while learning the material within. To access these features, go to **www.halleonard.com/mylibrary** and input the unique code printed on page 1 of this book.

CHAPTER 1
Basic Definitions

A few concepts form a common thread essential to the theoretical understanding of all music. These are defined below, assuming there is no existing knowledge of musical terms.

Pulse

Imagine a clock ticking. Usually, each tick will be separated from those before and after by exactly one second. Though you might play or sing complex, changing ideas against this regular ticking, and though they might seem to work either with or against it, the clock itself carries on unperturbed. This is the most basic representation of the term *pulse* in music.

Almost all music has a pulse, though it is not always in the foreground or entirely obvious. No matter how complex the other ingredients, pulse is the simplest defining feature of most pieces of music. Though it may speed up or slow down as the music develops, the underlying pulse is otherwise as simple as the ticking of a clock.

Tempo

Imagine that the clock in the above scenario could be adjusted so that the time interval between ticks—while still perfectly regular—could be set to any length. Instead of one tick per second, the ticking might be slowed down so that there was only one tick every two seconds; or sped up to produce several ticks per second. Fewer ticks in any given length of time would result in a slower pulse, while more ticks in the same time would be a faster pulse. Attempting to walk in time with each version would illustrate this effectively.

This relative speed of the pulse is known as *tempo*. Depending on the musical context, this may be described in general terms by using words, or, when wishing to be more precise, by using numbers.

Meter

Many clocks produce exactly the same sound for each tick. Imagine instead a clock with a pendulum producing a loud sound when swinging in one direction and a softer sound in the other direction: **loud**–soft–**loud**–soft–**loud**–soft.

Now, imagine instead that only one pulse in every three is emphasized: **loud**–soft–soft–**loud**–soft–soft–**loud**–soft–soft...

...Or one pulse in every four: **loud**–soft–soft–soft–**loud**–soft–soft–soft–**loud**–soft–soft–soft...

Any music created to be played in time with these differently organized pulses would tend to sound different because the repetition of musical ideas would mainly be organized to correspond to the cycle of strong and weak pulses.

This characteristic of music is known as *meter*. The examples above are defined as *duple*, *triple*, and *quadruple* meters (also known as duple, triple, or quadruple time).

Rhythm

Rhythm refers to the organization in time of musical elements within the overarching structure provided by pulse and, usually, meter. Imagine saying or rapping the following phrases repetitively over a constant pulse in duple meter:

- "Chicken in a box"
- "Duck-billed platypus"

Repeat both phrases, making sure that the italicized syllables coincide with the pulse (as they will naturally tend to):

"*Chick*-en in a *box*, *chick*-en in a *box*, *chick*-en in a *box*, *chick*-en in a *box*..."

The four syllables of "chicken in a" are equally distributed within a single pulse, while "box" gets a pulse to itself.

"*Duck*-billed *pla*-ty-pus, *duck*-billed *pla*-ty-pus, *duck*-billed *pla*-ty-pus, *duck*-billed *pla*-ty-pus..."

Here, "duck-billed" gets distributed equally within one pulse while the next pulse gets "platypus."

These two phrases, when delivered in this way, would be described as having different rhythms. Similarly, within a single piece of music, one instrument might play a part with few notes per pulse, while another might have a busier part with more notes per pulse. These components are also described as having different rhythms.

Pitch

Pitch describes the "highness" or "lowness" of a musical sound. This idea is generally understood by most, but the following examples may be imagined for clarity:

- The range of child's voice is generally higher than that of an adult.
- Adult male voices are generally lower pitched than adult female voices.
- An elephant's roar is lower pitched than the squeak of a mouse.
- Large instruments such as the double bass and tuba produce a lower range of pitches than smaller instruments such as the violin and flute.
- The notes of a piano, or other keyboard instruments, are usually ordered from the lowest at the extreme left to the highest at the extreme right.

Not all sounds used in music are described in terms of pitch. Percussive instruments, such as the many drums, cymbals, shakers, and tambourines, are not usually perceived as having pitch (though their sounds do in fact include pitched components). One of the basic classifications applied to musical instruments is therefore between pitched and unpitched instruments.

Timbre

Timbre describes the quality of a musical sound. The most basic classification here is between pitched and unpitched sounds. The sounds of pitched instruments may be further described using words such as smooth, harsh, mellow, piercing, hollow, and so on. This language is largely subjective, though more objective comparisons can be made by measuring various sonic properties. In general terms, timbre is the characteristic of a musical sound that usually lets us know immediately which instrument is making it.

Melody

A succession of differently pitched sounds is called a *melody*. Any given melody may be played or sung by any pitched instrument or voice and remain identifiable. Imagine any song you know played on a variety of different instruments. For example: "Three Blind Mice" played on the cello, piano, and xylophone. The melody remains identifiable as "Three Blind Mice" because the internal relationship between the pitches of its successive notes remains the same, regardless of the instrument or absolute pitch range used.

Harmony

Harmony describes the whole range of results and experiences when two or more pitched sounds are heard together and when this changes over time. The simplest possible event that could be described as an occurrence of harmony would be the sounding of two different pitches together followed by silence. If, instead of silence, one or both of the sounds changed in pitch, the result would be the simplest possible harmonic *progression*: a change in harmony over time.

Harmony is often described in terms of its relative simplicity or complexity. This is a product of the number of different pitches sounding at once, their relationship to each other, and the way these relationships change over time.

Musical Notation

Many systems exist to represent music graphically. At the simplest level, *musical notation* provides a series of instructions telling one or more performers what to play and when. Conventional notation systems usually represent pitch vertically against time, which is represented horizontally. Symbols representing musical notes are placed within this framework. If two or more notes are vertically aligned, they are therefore intended to sound simultaneously. As with Western written language, each page may contain several lines. Each line is read from left to right, and the lines are read from top to bottom.

Music for a single musician is known as a *part*; when several parts are shown together to represent an ensemble of two or more players, this is called a *score*. Here, the lines for each instrument are tied together, as shown below, to indicate that they are to be played simultaneously. As with vertically aligned notes in a single part, vertically aligned notes in different parts are also intended to be played simultaneously.

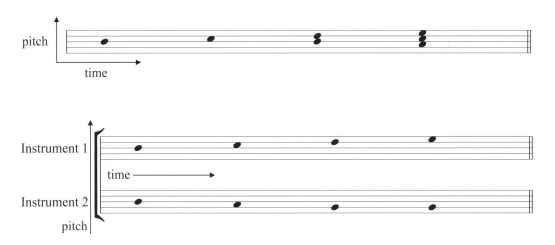

Notation systems do not only provide means of conveying instructions. For centuries, written music was the main tool used for the composition, dissemination, analysis, and evolution of musical language and ideas. Until the invention of sound recording, written music was the principle means by which a piece of music could be conceived, stored, and then reproduced. Composers and performers could be separated by both time and space—centuries and oceans—yet they could be reasonably sure that whole musical works would be conveyed as intended.

Musical notation has therefore evolved to a high level of complexity and sophistication. It would be difficult, if not impossible, to theorize about many aspects of music without it, and indeed much of the music we know simply would not have evolved. Nonetheless, it is important to remember that nothing you may see on a written or printed page is actually music; it is merely ink. The ink is only turned into music when it gives rise to sound, at which point it is heard and realized.

CHAPTER 2
Rhythm and Meter

In the most general sense, rhythm refers to the way in which sonic events are organized in relation to time. The sound associated with the motion of a train is often identifiably rhythmic, as individual sounds produced by various components are repeated within a cycle. The time interval between recurrences of the same sound in the cycle can often be perceived as the basic pulse of the rhythm. In contrast, the sounds of wind and rain are not usually identified as rhythmic, as they contain no such organized elements.

In musical notation, pulse and rhythm are shown by a number of devices, most fundamentally by organizing the music into *measures*.[1] Measures are separated by vertical lines called *bar lines*.

Within each measure, the next level of organization is the *beat*, or pulse. The number of beats per measure determines the meter: two beats per measure in duple time, three per measure in triple time, and so on.

In order to understand the symbols and terms used to define the meter and rhythms within it, we must first define a common set of note duration symbols. The longest and most fundamental of these in modern musical notation is the *whole note*.

WHOLE NOTE

All other note durations (or values) are defined in terms of their relation to the whole note, dividing by two to get each successive value; a whole note can be divided into two *half notes*, four *quarter notes*, eight *eighth notes*, and so on.

HALF NOTE   **QUARTER NOTE**   **EIGHTH NOTE**   **16th NOTE**

Note values are distinguished by the appearance of the *notehead*, whether or not they have stems, and whether or not they have tails or beams.

The notehead may be hollow or solid; only whole notes and half notes have hollow noteheads, while shorter values are solid. Only the whole note has no stem; all notes an eighth note or smaller have at least one tail, with one tail added for each halving of value. This progression has no theoretical limit (for example, a 512th note, if ever used, would have seven tails!), though values smaller than the 64th note are extremely rare.

It is important to note that, while there are many ways to define rhythms that divide the measure or pulse by any number (including odd numbers), note values themselves are only defined by halving. There is therefore no such thing as a third, fifth, or sixth note.

---

1   In British/International English, *bar* is used rather than measure; this is also generally understood in the USA.

Beaming

When notes an eighth note or smaller are used together (for example: four successive eighth or 16th notes), their tails are usually joined together to form beams for the sake of legibility.

Defining Meter

For any music with a regular pulse, a meter can be defined. As we have seen, this tells us how many pulses or beats are felt as a single cycle.

In written Western music, one of the most important symbols at the beginning of any piece is called the *time signature*,[2] which defines two important things about the meter: the number of beats per measure and the note value used to convey each beat.

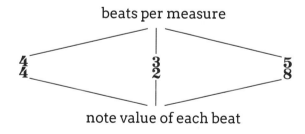

In speech, the examples of time signatures above translate into 4/4, 3/2, and 5/8 and convey that each measure would contain four quarter notes, three half notes, and five eighth notes, respectively.

---

2   In British/International English, the term "meter" itself is less frequently used by musicians; "time signature" is generally used to denote the meter and how it is notated.

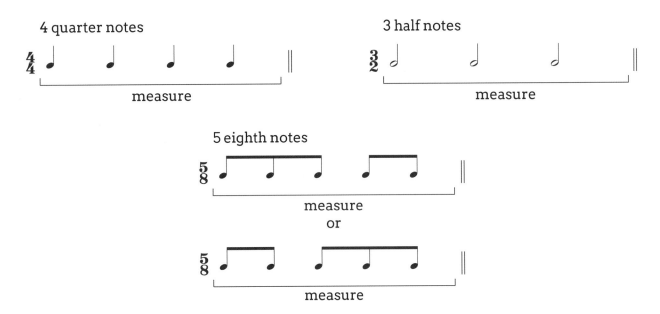

In theory, a measure may contain any number of beats, so the upper number may be any number from "1" upwards. In practice, a large majority of all written music has a two, three, or four here, but other numbers up to 15 are also encountered.

The lower number represents the note value used to write one beat (or pulse). Dividing this number into one gives you the note value (two gives 1/2, four gives 1/4, and so on). As the lower number corresponds to a note value that exists, only powers of two may be used: one, two, four, eight, 16, etc. Two, four, and eight are the most common, and anything beyond 16 is very rare.

The number "1" is rare in time signatures, though not impossible in either position. It is rarely seen as a number of beats per measure, as very little music has a pulse so insistent that it cannot be felt in groups of any kind. Here, it is most commonly encountered as a means of disrupting the meter by the addition of an extra beat. In the lower position, it would signify one whole note per beat, but this is not very useful as notes longer than one beat cannot be written simply.

Subdividing the Measure

The time signature defines the meter and the note values used to convey it, but the contents of a measure are not restricted to these note values alone. Longer values may be used to show notes of more than one beat's duration, while shorter values show subdivisions of the beat. The only unbreakable rule is that all the values used must add up to a total defined by the time signature. For example, a measure of 4/4 may contain one whole note, two half notes, four quarter notes, eight eighth notes, or 16 16th notes; it may also contain combinations such as a half note followed by two quarter notes, or two quarter notes followed by four eighth notes, and so on. The possible combinations are practically limitless.

The following rhythmic example in 4/4 contains many different valid combinations of note values within each measure.

TRACK 1

Reading Rhythms

The visual symbols in the previous example remain just that, unless they can be translated into rhythmically delivered sound, even if only in the imagination. To interpret the example, we must first remember that there are four quarter-note beats in each measure. We must then remember how many beats, or fractions of a beat, each note value corresponds to. If (and only if) the lower number in the time signature is four, we know the following:

- Whole notes are worth four beats each.

- Half notes arc two beats each.

- Quarter notes are one beat each.

- Eighth notes are half a beat each, so a group of two eighth notes is worth one beat.

- Sixteenth notes are worth a quarter of a beat each, so a group of four 16th notes is worth one beat.

TRACK 2

To tap the above rhythms correctly, first start counting "one, two, three, four" repeatedly at a steady tempo. The first measure (whole note) is represented by a single tap on beat 1, the second (half notes) by taps on beats 1 and 3, and so on. For the eighth and 16th notes, there should be two or four evenly spaced taps per beat.

This tapped rendition does not fully represent the way this would sound on any instrument capable of playing sustained notes as opposed to short taps. On an instrument such as a violin or flute (or the human voice), each note has a definite duration. To represent this, tap on every beat at a constant speed, singing or saying "la" to correspond with the length of each note.

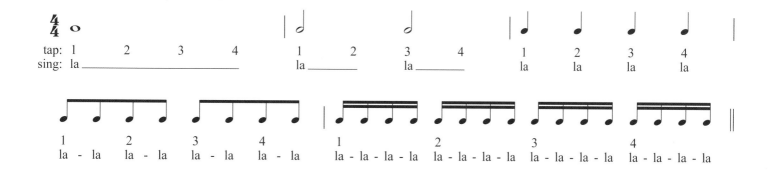

Various verbal devices can be used as a means of internalizing the common subdivisions of the beat, whatever the note values used to represent them. Half beats (represented by eighth notes in the examples here) may be verbalized by inserting "and" between beats: "one and two and three and four and." The next subdivision (quarter beats or 16th notes above) requires additional syllables, and is often rendered as, "1-e-and-a, 2-e-and-a, 3-e-and-a, 4-e-and-a."

Rests

Most music does not consist of an uninterrupted flow of notes from beginning to end. While this could be achieved on many instruments, it is impossible on others (wind instruments and the human voice require the player or singer to inhale occasionally). In any case, it is seldom desirable. Like human speech, most music is structured into phrases separated by silence.

In musical notation, these silences are represented by symbols called *rests*. While notes are instructions telling the player when and for how long to play each note, rests convey the corresponding instruction to *not* play and for how long. All note values have a corresponding rest value.

A measure of music may contain notes, rests, or any combination of the two. The total of all note and rest values in any measure must add up to match the time signature. In the following example, 3/4, the total of all note and rest values in each measure adds up to three quarter notes.

TRACK 3

Ties and Dotted Notes

In order to be able to notate any conceivable rhythm or length of note, a few additional devices are needed in addition to the basic note and rest values. The *tie* is a curved line which, as you might imagine, simply connects two or more notes together, combining their note values. This is particularly useful (indeed, essential) in order to write notes longer than a single measure in the current time signature, but it can also be used to create notes of any desired length within a single measure. The following example shows uses of the tie in 4/4.

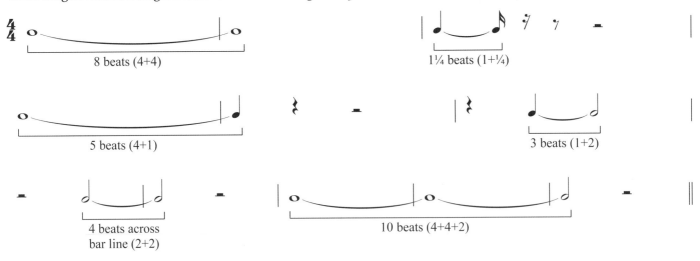

A *dot* placed after a note extends its value by half. This is equivalent to using a tie between two notes where one is twice the value of the other (2+1, 1+1/2, 1/2+1/4, etc.) but is often preferred as it is visually neater and easier to read. The following example shows uses of dotted notes in 3/4.

TRACK 4

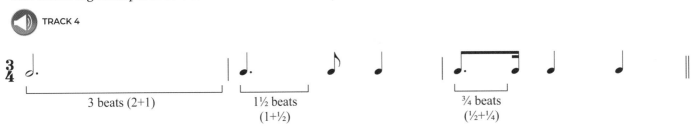

Double Dot

The principle of dotting may be extended further by using double dots. Here, the second dot extends the duration by half as much as the first dot. Therefore, a double-dotted quarter note would have the same duration as a quarter note plus an eighth note plus a 16th note. In terms of beats in 4/4: 1 + 1/2 + 1/4 = 3/4. Usually, doubling dotting is used if it simplifies the appearance of notes within a measure or beam group (see below).

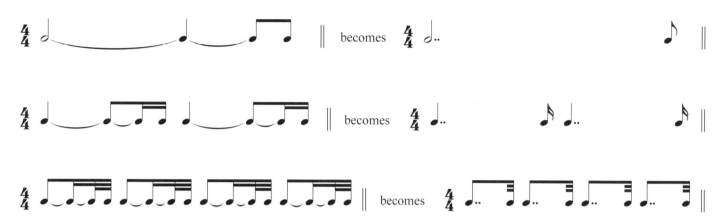

On each line above, the second measure shows the same rhythm as the first, but it's written using double dotting. In some these cases, this results in rhythms that are easier to read. The double dotting principle can, in theory, be extended to triple dots or beyond.

Other schools of thought advocate for outlining the beat division by the combination of ties and dots in lieu of the double-dot approach. Here are the examples above that have now been reformatted to show clear outlining of the beat division within the measure.

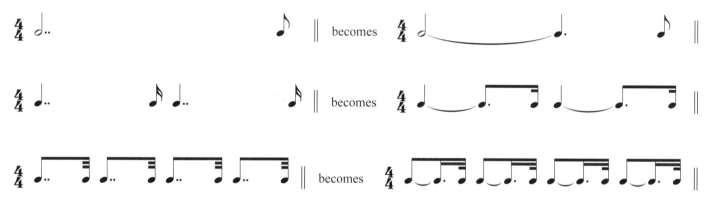

Triplets and Other Tuplets

Though note durations as defined by standard note values involve subdividing by powers of two (two, four, eight, 16, etc.), other durations are possible. The general term for a group of notes based on other subdivisions is *tuplets*. Tuplets may be defined by any numerical subdivision (three, five, six, seven, etc.); the most common of these is three. Notes derived from subdividing by three are called *triplets*.

🔊 TRACK 5

In the example above, each beat of the 4/4 pulse is divided by three, as indicated by the "3" above each beam group. In the absence of further information, the number above a tuplet group defines that there are that number of notes occurring at the same time as the number of notes of that value that would normally be beamed together. So the example above consists of eighth-note triplets; each beam group has three notes in the time of two.

In some instances, and for greater clarity, tuplets may be expressed as a ratio: two numbers separated by a colon, where the first defines the number in the group and the second the number of standard notes that add up to the same duration. The triplets above could therefore also be shown using "3:2" (three in the time of two). The second number is usually superfluous (and therefore omitted) but occasionally essential. In the examples below, it is easy to interpret the first group (quintuplets) as being five in the time of four, and the second (sextuplets) as being six in the time of four. This might be true for the final group too (septuplets: seven in the time of four) but because seven is so much closer to eight, they have been shown as a ratio for the avoidance of doubt.

Time Signatures in Use

Though many time signatures are theoretically possible, the majority of uses are covered by just a few of them. Firstly, humans tended to conceive music in either duple or triple time.[3] Other meters such as five or seven tend to sound unusual. Secondly, while the choice of a lower number (the note type defining the pulse) is entirely arbitrary on one level of theory, it has largely become governed by convention. In most styles, the quarter note is used to denote one beat.

The following time signatures are the most frequently encountered with a quarter note pulse, along with some recommended listening. Try to focus on the underlying pulse in each case rather than the intricacies of the melody line.

This is in many ways the simplest conceivable time signature. Some music written in 2/4 could equally well be written in 4/4 or 2/2 (see on the next page), but 2/4 generally implies that the pulse will not be felt in longer groupings, so consecutive 2/4 measures have equal weight. Because humans have two legs, this is very much akin to the rhythm established by walking or running; 2/4 time is often called *march time* as a result, and it is heavily used in marching band music.

Associated styles: march, polka, military two-step

Listening: Jimmy Shand & His Band: "Dashing White Sergeant"; Planxty: "Dennis Murphy's/The 42 Pound Cheque/John Ryan's Polka"

The first beat of each measure in 3/4 usually receives the greatest weight: "*one–two–three, one–two–three, one–two–three...*" It does not generally feel natural to walk or run in time to music in 3/4, partly because of this stress pattern and partly because it would be impossible to lead with the same foot in each measure. 3/4 time is often known as triple time, or *waltz time*, the waltz being a dance that reflects both of these issues; the dancers take one long, heavy step followed by two smaller lighter steps. This pattern is then repeated with the other foot leading and moving in the opposite direction.

Associated styles: waltz, country waltz/ballad, jazz waltz

Listening: Brahms: "16 Waltzes, Op. 39: No. 1 in B Major"; Miles Davis: "Some Day My Prince Will Come"; Patti Page: "Tennessee Waltz"

---

3   Four (quadruple) time is usually considered a variety of duple time because four is divisible by two and for other musical reasons explored in this chapter.

4/4 is easily the most common time signature in use, and it is in fact sometimes called *common time*. Used widely in rock and pop music, the iconic drummer's, "One, two, three, four!" count-in has entered the popular consciousness as the standard way to start a performance. Because four is a multiple of two, walking or running in time with music in 4/4 generally feels natural. Though some music in 4/4 could equally well be written in 2/4, in general, 4/4 reflects a hierarchy of emphasis where beat 1 is the heaviest, followed by beat 3, and then followed by beats 2 and 4, equally. In rock and pop music in 4/4, the thud of the bass drum usually defines beats 1 and 2, with the distinctive crack of the snare drum on beats 2 and 4. Listen to any of the rock examples below to illustrate this.

Associated styles: most Western music in many styles

Listening: Queen: "Another One Bites the Dust"; The Beatles: "I Saw Her Standing There"; Mozart: "Eine Kleine Nachtmusik (I: Allegro)"; James Brown: "Night Train"

5/4 time is a relatively rare time signature in any style of Western mainstream music, and somewhat challenging to walk, run, or dance to. For this reason, it is often associated with music of an exotic, unusual, or experimental nature.

Associated styles: modern jazz, progressive rock, world music, 20th century classical

Recommended listening: The Dave Brubeck Quartet: "Take Five"; Sting: "Seven Days"; Cream: "White Room" (intro only)

Half-Note Pulse Time Signatures

On one level, the time signatures of 2/4 and 2/2 can be seen as different ways of notating the same thing: two beats per measure. Whether half notes or quarter notes are used to denote the pulse (and therefore whether half beats are quarter notes or eighth notes, and so on...) could be seen as an arbitrary decision (or, in the days when it mattered, a case of saving time and valuable ink). In modern use, however, 2/2 time is strongly associated with certain styles, flavors, and tempos. Essentially, if the tempo of 4/4 is raised past a certain point, players will tend to stop feeling the music in four and instead feel two pulses in each measure as the dominant sense of pulse. Sometimes, either 4/4 or 2/2 could be used; in other cases, the choice is much more obvious. 2/2 is sometimes called *alla breve*, or alternatively, *cut time*, though this term and the associated symbol (₵) are now generally seen as old-fashioned.

Associated styles: musical theater, big band jazz, "light" orchestral music

Listening: Julie Andrews: "I Could Have Danced All Night" (from *My Fair Lady*); Tony Bennett and Count Basie: "Strike Up the Band"

3/2 time is rarely seen in popular music styles, but it is occasionally used to notate a slow triple time pulse in orchestral and choral music.

Compound Time

All the previously discussed time signatures are known as *simple* time signatures, meaning that the primary pulse (whatever the note value used to represent it) is further subdivided by halving. In 2/4, 3/4, and 4/4, quarter notes give the primary pulse but a secondary eighth-note pulse can be felt.

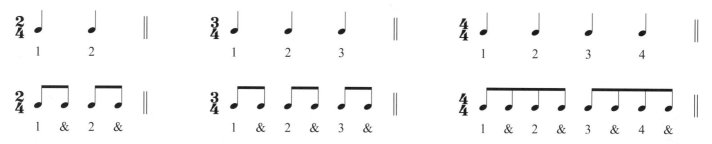

Compound time represents a different type of meter in which each primary pulse is divided into three instead of two. The secondary pulse is usually represented by eighth notes. As three eighth notes add up to the same duration as a dotted quarter note, this is used for the primary pulse.

Because the lower number in a conventional time signature has to represent a simple note value ("dotted quarter note" is not a simple value), eight is used as the lower number to denote compound time signatures, even though this represents the secondary rather than primary pulse. Two, three, and four, respectively multiplied by three, gives six, nine, and 12. 6/8, 9/8, and 12/8 are therefore the compound time signatures that correspond to 2/4, 3/4, and 4/4 in simple time.

Compound time signatures may, in a sense, be viewed as the "triplety" versions of simple time signatures; on one level, anything written in 12/8 could equally well be written in 4/4 with triplets, but the use of compound time implies that the subdivision by three is the norm for the piece rather than an exception. Sometimes, this distinction can be a little blurred and the decision is arbitrary.

Associated styles: Irish jig, Baroque gigue, classical, pop ballads

Recommended listening: The Bothy Band: "The Kesh Jig" (6/8); The Cardigans: "If There Is a Chance" (9/8); J.S. Bach: "Partita II for Solo Violin—Gigue" (12/8); Elvis Presley: "Can't Help Falling in Love" (12/8)

Note Grouping and Beaming Conventions

Eighth notes and shorter notes are encountered both individually (with tails) and in groups, where they are usually joined by beams. While it is possible to group beamed notes together in almost any combination, certain conventions prevail for most cases. In general terms, the goal is twofold: to maximize legibility and to reflect the musical grammar and intention within the musical material. Usually, beaming groups should reflect, or at least not contradict, the underlying pulse of the time signature.

Eighth notes in simple time may be beamed across two beats (though not across the halfway point in the measure). Apart from this, the first note in each beamed group usually shows where the beat lies. The following measures in 4/4 contain conventionally beamed groups of eighth and 16th notes.

The following example shows a measure of 4/4 beamed in two different ways. The second measure is considered unconventional because the beaming crosses the halfway point in the measure (also known as the *invisible bar line*).

The following measure shows possible combinations of eighths and 16ths in 4/4, with beaming showing each beat.

The following measure shows combinations of eighth, 16th, and 32nd notes. Again, the first note on each beat is clearly identifiable as the first of a beamed group.

In compound time, beaming should reflect the primary (dotted quarter note) pulse. The following measures show conventional beaming of various combinations of eighth, 16th, and 32nd notes within the 12/8 time signature:

When notes are grouped like this, the primary pulse is easy to identify; just look for the first note of each beamed group. Again, this is a matter of musical logic as well as legibility.

Like many other rules in music, these beaming conventions are not unbreakable. When it occurs, beaming across the pulse is usually done in order to outline an alternative pulse (see Glossary: *Cross-Rhythm*).

Tempo

One of the defining characteristics of any piece of music is its *tempo*, or speed. For centuries, composers' intentions were described in words only. While the use of any language is, of course, legitimate (especially the composer's own), the vast bulk of all published music uses one of three languages for tempo: German, English, and, especially, Italian. Italian tempo directions are the most widely recognized, internationally.

Since the invention of the metronome,[4] followed by more recent technology, including drum machines and computer-based audio recording, the number-based tempo system has gradually gained ground in contemporary classical music as well as all forms of popular music.

In both systems, the tempo direction usually refers to the primary pulse (for example, quarter notes in 4/4 or dotted quarter notes in 6/8) which is then either described using one or more words or defined in terms of *beats per minute* (often abbreviated to *bpm*).

Tempo instructions are usually given at the start of a piece and again if the tempo changes. Some examples are shown below:

Allegro	Italian: fast
Langsam	German: slowly
Very Fast	
♩ = 100	100 quarter notes per minute
♩. = 80	80 dotted quarter notes per minute
♩ = 150	150 half notes per minute

---

4   A mechanical or electronic device used to generate a regular rhythmic pulse at a precisely defined tempo. Used for practice and reference.

The use of words rather than numbers is inevitably less precise, though this may be seen as an advantage, allowing musicians and conductors greater freedom in their interpretation. Nonetheless, some consensus exists around the approximate correspondence between Italian tempo markings and beats per minute. Approximate bpm values for some of the most frequently encountered Italian terms are given below.

- *Lento* (slowly): 40–60bpm

- *Largo* (slowly): 40–60bpm

- *Adagio* (at ease): 66–76bpm

- *Andante* (walking pace): 76–108bpm

- *Moderato* (moderately): 108–120bpm

- *Allegro* (fast): 120–168bpm

- *Vivace* (lively): 168–176bpm

- *Presto* (very fast): 168–200bpm

- *Prestissimo* (extremely fast): more than 200bpm

CHECKPOINT 1
Basics and Rhythms

1. The note values below have been shuffled into a random order. Identify them by name and by the number of beats represented in 4/4.

2. This exercise contains empty measures in various time signatures. Fill each measure using the correct number of each note value.

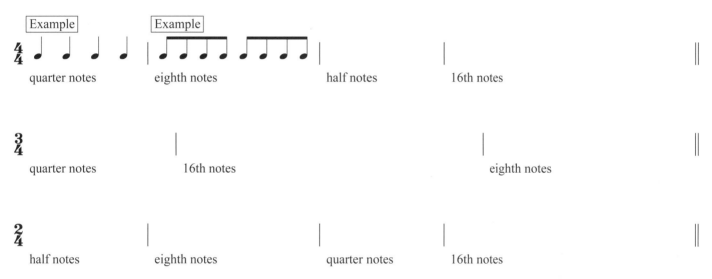

3. In each line of music below, one measure is incorrect; the note and rest values do not add up to the total specified in the time signature. Identify the measure in question within each line.

4. The following examples in 4/4 and 6/8 contain unbeamed eighth and 16th notes. Rewrite them with standard beaming.

5. The following example contains some tied notes that could have been written as higher note values or dotted notes, and others that should remain as ties. Rewrite as appropriate.

6. Listen to the following songs/pieces in the first column carefully and rearrange the time signatures in the second column so they match.

Seal: "Kiss from a Rose"	$\frac{4}{4}$
Robert Palmer: "Addicted to Love"	$\frac{5}{4}$
Paul Simon: "Have a Good Time"	$\frac{3}{4}$
Holst: "Mars, the Bringer of War" (from *The Planets*)	$\frac{6}{8}$
Pat Metheny & Charlie Haden: "Spiritual"	$\frac{7}{4}$

7. Using a metronome, app, or any software with a "tap tempo" function,[5] find and write down a tempo for each of the following songs/pieces. Your results may be slightly approximate, but this is less important than developing a working feel for various tempo ranges.

    MC5: "Sister Anne"

    Chic: "Le Freak"

    Charlie Parker: "Donna Lee"

    The Blue Nile: "Over the Hillside"

    Neil Young: "Only Love Can Break Your Heart"

    Taylor Swift/Bon Iver: "Exile"

    Green Day: "Basket Case"

    James Taylor: "Music"

    Philip Glass: "Glassworks I—Opening"

---

5   This useful functionality does exactly what it says, and it is available in many free apps as well as most recording software. Simply keep tapping in the tempo for a readout.

CHAPTER 3
Pitch

Sound is caused by vibrations, whether of an instrument string, reed, vocal cord, loudspeaker diaphragm, or any other physical object. These vibrations cause corresponding movements (*sound waves*) in the air, and then physical vibrations in the complex apparatus within our ears. This is decoded by our brains and experienced as the phenomenon we know as sound.

Many kinds of associated information are extracted from this sound by brains, including speech patterns, instrument timbres, localization (which direction the sound is coming from), and *pitch*. We experience pitch as "highness" versus "lowness." This is, in fact, directly related to the frequency of the sound waves, or the number of vibrations per second in the source of the sound. Simply put, the faster the sound-producing object vibrates, the higher the pitch of sound we experience. Human hearing can detect sounds with frequencies as low as approximately twenty cycles per second (using expressed as 20 Hertz or Hz) and up to approximately 20,000 cycles per second (20 kilohertz, or kHz).[6]

If two different sounds are perceived as having different pitches, it is because they have different frequencies. The relationship between these frequencies determines our perception of how far apart the pitches are, whether they seem to belong together musically, and if so, whether combining them seems pleasant (*consonant*) or unpleasant (*dissonant*) to the ear.

If two pitches have frequencies in the ratio 2:1 (so that one pitch has twice the frequency of the other), they combine with the most consonant result possible; they are considered so alike that they are given the same note name (see below). All notes sharing the same note name are said to belong to the same *pitch class*.

Dividing the Octave

If two pitches an octave apart produce the greatest possible consonance, it follows that there are notes in between which combine with varying degrees of consonance and dissonance. There are many systems worldwide for dividing the octave and classifying the resulting pitches. These play a large part in defining the ways in which some folk music traditions around the world sound so radically different to Western music and to each other.

Modern Western music is based on the division of the octave into 12 equal intervals, meaning that the frequency ratio[7] between two consecutive notes is always the same. The interval between two consecutive notes in this system is called a *half step, half tone*, or *semitone*. On a piano or keyboard instrument, this is the interval between any two adjacent keys (whether white or black); on the guitar and other fretted instruments, it is the interval between any two adjacent frets on the same string. It is generally considered the most dissonant interval within the octave.

As you might imagine, the interval spanning two half tones is called a *whole tone* or a *whole step*, or simply a *tone*. Together, tones and half tones are the basic building blocks of Western music.

The first seven letters of the alphabet are used as the basis for naming all notes within the octave. This pattern repeats so that any notes an octave apart always share the same name. Seven of the unique notes within each octave are named using letter names only: A, B, C, D, E, F, and G. These are the white notes on the piano keyboard.

---

6   The upper threshold of human pitch perception falls with age and exposure to high sound pressure levels.

7   The ratio in question is $1:2^{1/12}$ (one to the 12th root of two).

The remaining five notes in each octave—the black notes on the keyboard—are named with reference to the white notes, by means of the suffixes *sharp* (meaning "raised by a half tone") and *flat* (meaning "lowered by a half tone"). The note between A and B can therefore be called "A sharp" or "B flat" depending on context. Alternative names for the same physical note are known as *enharmonic equivalents*. It is very important to note that in most contexts, only one of the two possible note names is considered correct.

"Sharp" and "flat" are usually denoted using the symbols ♯ (sharp) and ♭ (flat). In text, these are placed after the letter name: A♯ (A sharp), B♭ (B flat), C♯ (C sharp), D♭ (D flat), and so on.

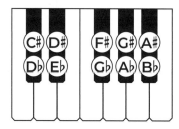

Note that there is no black note between the pairs B–C and E–F. Alternatively, remember that all other adjacent pairs of white notes are a whole tone apart.

Sometimes, it is necessary to clarify that a particular note is neither a sharp nor a flat. The suffix *natural* (or ♮ in symbol form) is used to denote this: C♮ (C natural), F♮ (F natural), and so on.

The Stave

The most common system used to represent pitch in modern musical notation is the five-line *stave*, or *staff*.

Notes are placed either between lines or on a line (which actually means that the line bisects the notehead).

Notes between lines:

Notes on lines:

As the stave does not in itself allow for a very large pitch range, notes may also be placed just above or below the stave (as though in the space between the outermost line and another, imaginary line), or on a temporary enlargement of the stave made possible by the use of *ledger lines*.

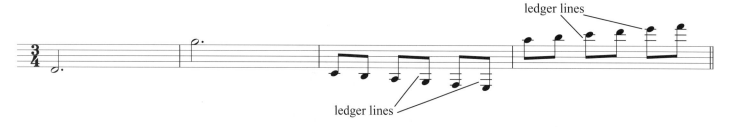

Notes on or below the middle line are usually written with tails pointing up, while notes on or above the middle line are shown with tails down, though there are many situations in which this is varied.

Clefs

The number of notes within the combined range of commonplace instruments and voices is too large to be accommodated by this system alone, at least not without using a very large number of ledger lines (which becomes increasingly difficult to sightread, among other disadvantages). The use of a *clef* provides a simple solution to this issue. Placed at the start of each line of music (and sometimes elsewhere if a change of range is required), the clef defines the pitch range in use, normally in such a way that the core range of the instrument or voice for which the music is intended falls in and around the stave without requiring a great number of ledger lines. The clef establishes that a given line represents a certain pitch; the pitches represented by all other lines and spaces relate to this reference point.

Clefs are usually either known by a name or by the note they represent. Since each clef symbol is known by several names, depending on the line on which is is placed, it is most useful to first learn the note represented by each clef. As a point of reference, we will relate these to their position on the piano keyboard.

The C note nearest to the middle of the piano keyboard is known as *middle C*; the *C clef* establishes that the line on which it is placed will be middle C. The *G clef* similarly identifies the line on which it placed as the G above middle C; the *F clef* is used to locate the F below middle C.

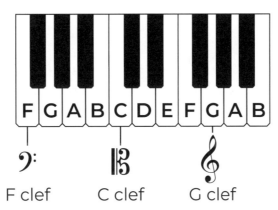

Treble Clef

The G clef is very rarely seen anywhere other than the second line up. For this reason, the terms G clef and *treble clef* are essentially synonymous. The resulting notes on the stave up to four ledger lines in either direction are shown below.

Instruments/voices associated with the treble clef: female voices, violin, guitar, upper wind and brass instruments, and *lead sheets*.[8]

Bass Clef

The F clef is similarly almost always placed on the second line down, where it is known as the *bass clef*. As its name implies, this makes it useful for instruments and voice with a relatively low pitch range.

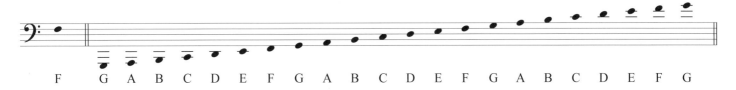

Instruments/voices associated with the bass clef: cello, double bass, bass guitar, bassoon, trombone, and tuba.

---

8   A common form of notation used in jazz and pop music, where the melody is notated with chord symbols for unspecified instruments/voices.

Alto Clef

The C clef is usually placed on one of two lines. On the middle line, it is known as the *alto clef*. It is almost exclusively associated with the viola.

Instruments/voices associated with the alto clef: viola and alto trombone.

Tenor Clef

When placed on the second line down, the C clef is called the *tenor clef*.

The tenor clef is generally used for the upper ranges of bass clef instruments including cello, bassoon, and trombone. It should be noted that the notes on the ledger lines below the stave here are largely redundant; parts for these instruments generally use the bass clef for this range.

The Piano Stave

The piano has a far greater pitch range than most other instruments, and can also simultaneously produce notes that are far apart; the left hand may routinely play the very lowest notes while the right hand plays the very highest. In order to accommodate this range, both hands playing up to ten notes at once, and rhythmic independence between hands, a single stave and clef are insufficient. Music for piano and other keyboard instruments is therefore generally written on two staves, with the bass clef used for the left hand while the right hand is shown on the treble clef (this also known as the *grand staff*).

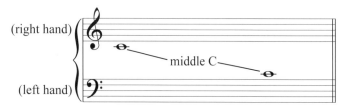

Note that middle C is shown on the first ledger line below the treble clef and the first ledger line above the bass clef as usual; the use of more ledger lines therefore allows for a considerable overlap between the ranges covered by each hand. Care should be taken not to accidentally require both hands to play the same note, or to overlap in a physically difficult way. Most of the time, the area around middle C will be where the hands meet, but occasionally either hand may play outside of its usual zone; in these cases a temporary bass or treble clef may be used on either stave.

The piano stave may also be also used to represent an entire instrumental or vocal ensemble, whether or not the result is intended to be played on the piano. This is called a *reduction* or *short score*.

Sharps, Flats, and Key Signatures

The five-line stave may be used to show any note, whether natural, flat, or sharp. By default, a note is assumed to be a natural. Sharps and flats are indicated in one of two ways: *accidentals* and *key signatures*.

Accidentals

A sharp or flat symbol may be placed immediately to the left of any note.

The notes above are therefore F#, B♭, C#, and E♭, as are any further notes on the same line or space within the same measure.

Key Signatures

One or more sharp or flat symbols may be placed on specific lines or spaces at the beginning of each line in a piece of music (directly after the clef) to indicate they apply throughout the piece. This also indicates the musical key of the piece, discussed later in the book.

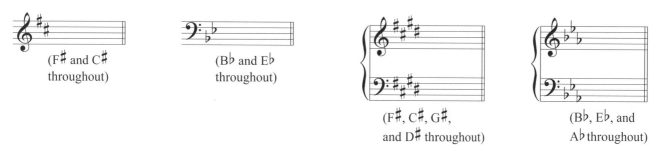

A number of general rules apply to accidentals and keys signatures:

- Sharps and flats specified by the key signature apply to all octaves, not just those shown.

TRACK 6

- Sharps and flats in a key signature remain in force unless superseded by a new key signature or are temporarily suspended by accidentals.

- A conventional key signature may contain sharps, flats, or neither, but not both.

- A natural may be used as an accidental if a sharp or flat is specified in the key signature. For example, in order to write an F natural where F# has been specified by the key signature, the natural symbol (♮) must be used as an accidental.

TRACK 7

- An accidental remains in force for the rest of the measure unless contradicted later. For example, to write a B♮ later in a measure where a B♭ has been used, the natural symbol must be used as an accidental.

- An accidental remains in force if a note is tied across a bar line.

TRACK 8

- *Courtesy accidentals* are often used as a reminder to return to the key signature in the measure after an accidental has been used. In the example below, where an F natural is indicated as an accidental and an F♯ is intended in the following measure, this is shown as an accidental for the avoidance of doubt. There is some variation in this practice; some composers and publishers do not use courtesy accidentals at all, while others place them in parentheses.

- Accidentals are usually held to apply only in the octave where they are used, but courtesy accidentals are usually used for the avoidance of doubt where a note of the same letter name occurs in a different octave either simultaneously or later in the measure.

Enharmonic Equivalence

As we have seen, the "black" notes have alternative names (A♯=B♭, C♯=D♭, etc.). This concept, known as *enharmonic equivalence*, can also apply to the "white" notes, for reasons which will become clear as more advanced areas of theory are explored.

As there are no black notes between B and C or between E and F, it would seem fair to suppose that the notes B♯, C♭, E♯, and F♭ do not exist at all. In fact, as sharp simply means "raised by a half step" and flat means "lowered by a half step," these notes do exist: B♯ is in fact the same physical note as C. In the same way, B and C♭ are equivalent, as are E and F♭, and E♯ and F.

Double Sharps and Double Flats

As their names would suggest, *double sharps* and *double flats* raise and lower the pitch of a note by two half steps (a whole tone), respectively. This means that most double sharps and double flats are in fact white notes, and the enharmonic equivalents of naturals. For example, F double sharp is the enharmonic equivalent of G natural, while G double flat is equivalent to F natural.

Double sharps and double flat symbols function very similarly to regular sharps and flats in most respects, and are shown on the stave and in text using the following symbols:

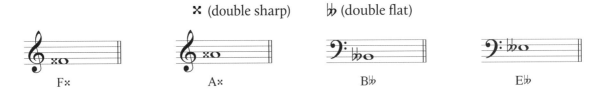

8va and 8vb

Notes requiring many ledger lines can be difficult to sightread, and create layout issues in parts and scores. There are several ways to solve this. On some instruments (such as cello and piano) changes of clef are used routinely; the treble clef may be used for the piano's left hand when accessing high notes, and equally, the right hand may use bass clef. High notes on the cello are usually written using tenor clef.

The more universal solution is the use of octave transposition symbols. These literally mean "play this note an octave higher/lower than written."

- 8va: play an octave higher (Italian: *ottava*)
- 8vb: play an octave lower (Italian: *ottava bassa*)

Occasionally, the symbols 15ma and 15vb are used to mean two octaves up or down respectively (because a 15th is two octaves).

Scientific Pitch Notation

There are many ways to describe pitches in text form using absolute terms; sometimes we need to give not only the name of the note, but its range. Middle C is often used as a reference, so a note may be described as "C above middle C" or "F three octaves below middle C." This can often result in confusion, however.

Scientific pitch notation is more reliable, and establishes middle C as C4; the C above this is C5 and C below is C3. There is very rarely any need to use negative numbers as these frequencies are inaudible.

Other notes are numbered in relation to the C below. For example, the A above middle C is A4.

<table>
<tr><td colspan="3">

Instrument Ranges

It is useful to have an idea of the ranges of common instruments and voices. The following list is intended as a reference. Highest notes (and sometimes lowest notes) are often somewhat arbitrary.

</td></tr>
<tr><td>Piano: A0–C8</td><td>Clarinet: E3–C7</td><td>Harp: B♭0–G♯7</td></tr>
<tr><td>Double Bass: E1–A4</td><td>Bassoon: B♭1–E5</td><td>Acoustic Guitar: E2–C6</td></tr>
<tr><td>Cello: C2–E6</td><td>Trumpet: F♯3–F♯6</td><td>Electric Guitar: E2–D6</td></tr>
<tr><td>Viola: C3–E7</td><td>Trombone: C2–C5</td><td>Bass Guitar: E1–C4</td></tr>
<tr><td>Violin: G3–B7</td><td>French Horn: C2–C6</td><td>Voices: see Chapter 11</td></tr>
<tr><td>Flute: C4–E7</td><td>Tuba: E♭2–A4</td><td></td></tr>
<tr><td>Oboe: B♭3–B♭6</td><td>Pipe Organ: C0–C9</td><td></td></tr>
</table>

TOOLBOX

CHECKPOINT 2
Pitch

1. Label all the notes on the keyboard below. Black notes should be labelled with both possible names.

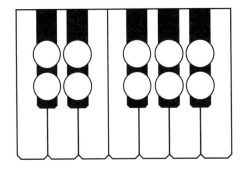

2. Label the notes shown below on the treble, bass, and alto clefs. The first note for each clef is given. For the purposes of this exercise, sharp and flat symbols only affect the notes to which they are attached; all others should be assumed to be naturals.

3. Add the notes given below the stave to each line below, alternating between ascending and descending motion.

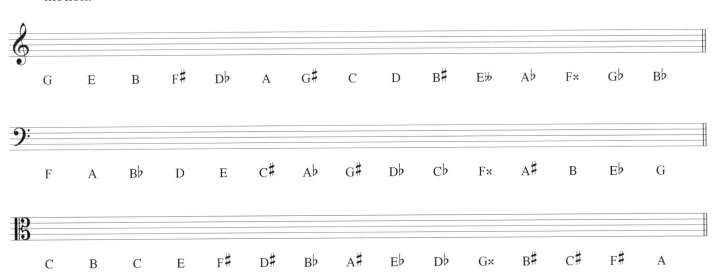

4. Rewrite the following melodies in a different clef as specified. The result does not have to be in the same octave, as long as the note names are the same and the direction of motion is preserved (e.g., C in the treble clef becomes a C somewhere in the bass clef and the melody rises or falls to give it the same overall shape).

CHAPTER 4
Scales and Keys

Western music is built around a few central ideas. The related concepts of scale, key, and tonality are among the most important.

Though the octave is divided into 12 equal steps, very little music has been written where all 12 notes have equal importance all of the time; the results are instantly identifiable as distinctly avant-garde[9] and not intended as relaxing or pleasant. Most music is *tonal* at least most of the time, meaning that it has a key center and tonality. Let's try to define these terms without going around in circles.

When music is made using fewer than all 12 notes, it can usually be said to have a *key*. This is a family of notes (usually seven) that define both the essential character of the music (its *tonality*) and the central note (*key center*) around which this is built. The tonality of most tonal music is either *major* or *minor*, and the key center may be any one of the twelve notes of the octave. These properties are usually denoted together: C major, E♭ major, D minor, and F♯ minor are all examples of keys.

In the major/minor key system, seven notes per octave go together to define any given key. When played ascending and descending by stepwise motion, this is called a *scale*. For example, the key of C major is defined by the C major scale. This may be examined in some detail to show the important properties of the major scale so that we may then apply them to other key centers.

The *major scale* is an arrangement of whole tones and half tones.

(W = whole, H = half)

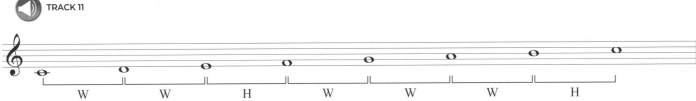

This arrangement (convenient to memorize in two halves: "whole, whole, half; whole, whole, whole, half") gives the major scale and anything written in a major key its characteristic sound. This is fairly well ingrained into the Western consciousness even among non-musicians, not least because of Julie Andrews' rendition of "Do-Re-Mi" in *The Sound of Music*.[10] Though this is a generalization, the sound of major tonality is often described as happy.

The notes of the C major scale define the key of C major. One reason for practicing scales is to make it easy to play pieces written in their respective keys. The key and scale of C major are generally viewed as "easy" because all of their notes are naturals, as opposed to sharps or flats.

To construct the major scale from any key center other than C, the same pattern ("whole, whole, half; whole, whole, whole, half") must be applied from a different starting point. In order to preserve this arrangement, all major scales other than C must contain one or more sharps or flats. This becomes obvious if we attempt to construct a major scale starting on G, using only naturals.

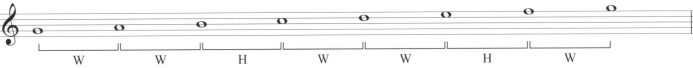

---

9   See Glossary: *atonality, serialism.*
10   See Glossary: *solfege.*

As the interval between E and F is only a half tone, and we require a whole tone between the sixth and seventh steps, the seventh note must be F♯ rather than F. This establishes that the key of G major is defined as having one sharp (F♯).

TRACK 13

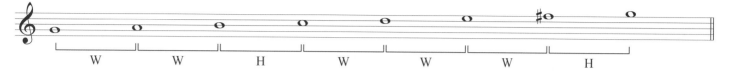

As we have seen, the number of sharps or flats (or none) at the start of each line of music establishes which notes are sharps or flats unless cancelled by accidentals; in so doing it also established the key. From the information above, we can define two key signatures: C major (no sharps or flats) and G major (one sharp).

It is worth noting at this point that if a conventional key signature has only one sharp, it can only be an F♯. Any other single sharp would result in a distribution of whole/half steps other than the required pattern. While the result might be musically interesting, it would not be a major scale. Similarly, if there are two sharps, they can only be F♯ and C♯. This establishes the key of D major.

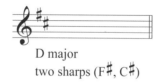

The Circle of Fifths: Sharp Keys

Music is full of interesting patterns. One of these is apparent here. We moved five steps up the scale of C major (C, D, E, F, G) in order to start building a major scale on G. This required the use of F♯, which is a half step below G, and the seventh step of the G major scale. Moving another five steps (G, A, B, C, D) to the next key center results in the addition of C♯, which is a half step below D, and the seventh note of the D major scale.

This establishes a pattern: We can keep moving up five steps to a new key, and keep adding sharps; the last sharp to be added is always a half step below the key center. As this always appears as the rightmost sharp symbol in the key signature, it can very easily be used to identify any major key with sharps. This progression is an example of a *circle of fifths* (or *cycle of fifths*). Here's the full cycle of fifths for "sharp" key signatures:

Note that the last two sharps to be added (E♯ and B♯) are actually white notes on the keyboard: the enharmonic equivalents of F and C, respectively. However, one of the important principles of the major/minor key system is that in any scale, each letter must be used only once per octave. The seventh step of the F♯ major scale *must* be some kind of E as the letter F is already taken; therefore, it can only be E♯.

Flat Keys

What if, instead of moving five steps up from C major, we moved five steps down? This would take us to the new key center of F. Attempting to construct a major scale on F using only naturals would result in a similar issue as G; the note B natural does not belong. To preserve the major scale pattern, it must be changed to B♭. Thus the key signature of F major has one flat (B♭).

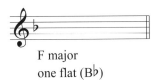

F major
one flat (B♭)

Just as with the sharp keys, we can continue in this way to produce the next flat key. Moving five steps down the F major scale, we arrive at B♭. In this new key, it is again the fourth step which must be flatted: from E to E♭. Continuing this pattern produces the rest of the flat keys.

The flats are also added in a useful sequence for memorizing key signatures; the penultimate flat symbol (second from the right) in all of the flat keys from B♭ major onwards tells us the name of the key. For example, the key signature with three flats (B♭, E♭, and A♭) is E♭ major; five flats (B♭, E♭, A♭, D♭, and G♭) is D♭ major.

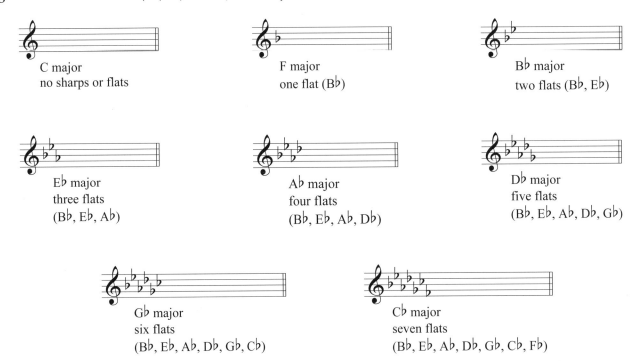

C major
no sharps or flats

F major
one flat (B♭)

B♭ major
two flats (B♭, E♭)

E♭ major
three flats
(B♭, E♭, A♭)

A♭ major
four flats
(B♭, E♭, A♭, D♭)

D♭ major
five flats
(B♭, E♭, A♭, D♭, G♭)

G♭ major
six flats
(B♭, E♭, A♭, D♭, G♭, C♭)

C♭ major
seven flats
(B♭, E♭, A♭, D♭, G♭, C♭, F♭)

As in the final two sharp keys, the final two flat keys introduce flats which are actually "white" key notes. C♭ is enharmonically equivalent to B, while F♭ is the same note as E. Just as with sharp keys, the "one letter name per step" rule dictates that they must be named as they are.

Note also that the final two sharp and flat keys are actually the same: G♭ is enharmonically F♯, and C♭ is enharmonically B. It may seem that deciding whether to write in one of two enharmonically equivalent keys is entirely arbitrary, but there are usually contextual reasons for preferring one over the other.

The sharp keys and flat keys can therefore be viewed as one complete circle where the "far" sharp and flat keys overlap.

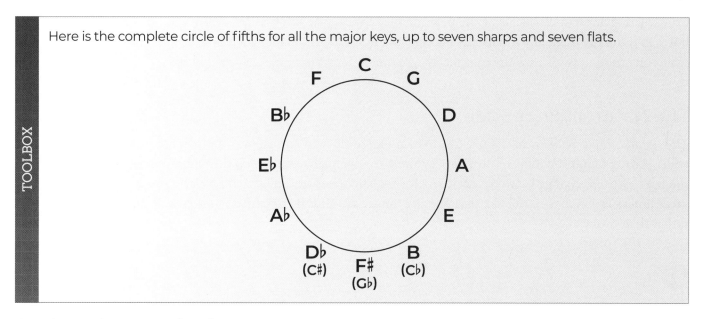

Here is the complete circle of fifths for all the major keys, up to seven sharps and seven flats.

Scale Step Terminology

The seven steps of the major scale are important reference terms in music theory, particularly when describing harmony. While modern numerals are used in a number of other contexts, scale steps (and chords built on them) are described either with words or Roman numerals, as follows:

I   *tonic*
II   *supertonic*
III *mediant*
IV   *subdominant*
V   *dominant*
VI   *submediant*
VII *leading note*

Minor Scales and Keys

In the major/minor key system, for every major key, there is a corresponding *minor* key which shares its key signature. This can be found by counting three steps (inclusive) downwards from the tonic of the major key. For example, from C major we would count "C, B, A" and arrive at the note A and the key of A minor; from the key of A♭ major we would count "A♭, G, F" and arrive at F minor.

This is a relative relationship: A minor is the relative minor of C major; C major is the relative major of A minor.

Constructing any major scale using the notes defined by a key signature is a simple matter of stepping through the notes in order, through any number of octaves; the notes are the same whether ascending or descending. Minor scale construction is a little more complicated, as the minor scale can take several forms.

The Natural Minor Scale

The *natural minor scale* is the simplest form of minor scale, and corresponds most directly to the relative major scale. Having found the tonic of the relative minor key, we again simply step through the notes from one tonic to the next, with no change between ascending forms. The notes of C major and A natural minor are therefore the same notes. To emphasize the fact that A is the tonic note and the tonality is minor, we simply play from A to A rather than C to C.

TRACK 14

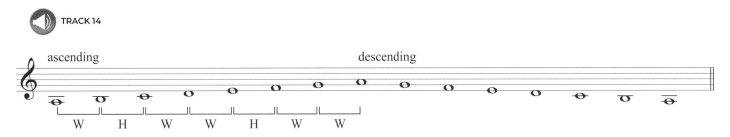

Though these are again generalizations, minor tonality is often described as sounding sad where the major is happy. Compared to other minor scales, the natural minor scale is sometimes described as sounding folky.

The Harmonic Minor Scale

In Western classical music, the minor scale can take various other forms which are modified versions of the natural minor scale. The *harmonic minor scale* can be viewed as the set of notes from which minor key harmony is mainly built, and is derived by raising the seventh degree of the scale by a half step using an accidental. For example, the seventh step of the A natural minor scale is G natural. To create A harmonic minor this is changed to G♯. Likewise, the seventh step of F natural minor is E♭. To arrive at F harmonic minor, this is changed to E natural.

The interval between the sixth and seventh steps of the harmonic minor scale spans three half steps and is called an *augmented second*. This interval gives the harmonic minor scale its characteristic sound, which is often described as "Spanish."

TRACK 15

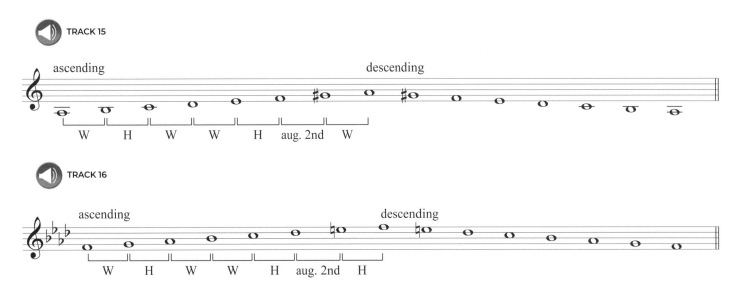

TRACK 16

The Melodic Minor Scale

In minor tonality, melodic writing often uses a slightly different set of notes depending on whether the line is ascending or descending. This is expressed as a scale with different ascending and descending forms. In the ascending form of the *melodic minor scale*, both the sixth and seventh steps of the natural minor scale are raised by a half step; these revert to the natural minor in the descending form. For example, in A melodic minor, the sixth and seventh ascending steps are F♯ and G♯; in the descending form these revert to naturals (F and G). In F harmonic minor, the sixth and seventh steps are D natural and E natural; these revert to the flats in the key signature (D♭ and E♭) in the descending form.

TRACK 17

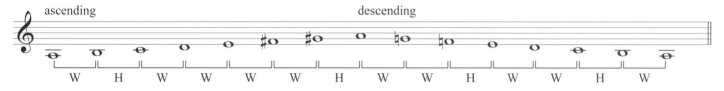

TRACK 18

The Melodic Minor Scale in Jazz

A significant amount of modern jazz theory is derived from the melodic minor scale. In this context, only the ascending form of the classical melodic minor scale is used, so the sixth and seventh steps remain raised when descending. The resulting scale is usually known as *jazz melodic minor*, *jazz minor*, or sometimes (by jazz theorists!) the *real* melodic minor scale.

TRACK 19

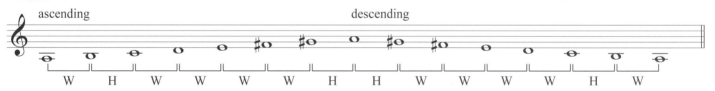

TRACK 20

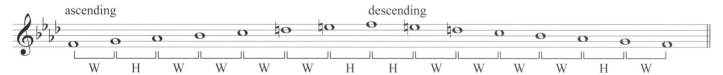

Relative vs. Parallel Minor

Relative major and minor scales or keys share a key signature, and are therefore derived from the same set of notes; the main difference is the key center or tonic note. It can also be useful to compare major and minor scales in a different way: by relating the major and various minor scales that can be built from the same tonic note. For example, let's compare the C major scale with the various C minor scales. To do this, the major scale is used as the reference point, with its notes labelled from 1 to 7:[11]

TRACK 21

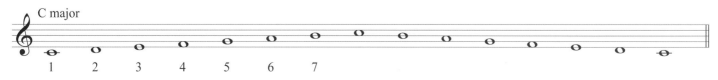

---

11   In this context, modern numerals (as used here) may be encountered rather than Roman numerals.

The various C minor scales may be defined as parallel (rather than relative) to C major, noting which steps in each case are the same, and which differ. All minor scales may therefore be viewed as having a flatted third compared with the parallel major. In the case of the jazz melodic minor scale, this is the only difference. The natural minor (and descending form of the classical melodic minor) also has flatted sixth and seventh steps, compared with the major. Harmonic minor has the flatted sixth but not seventh.

 TRACK 22

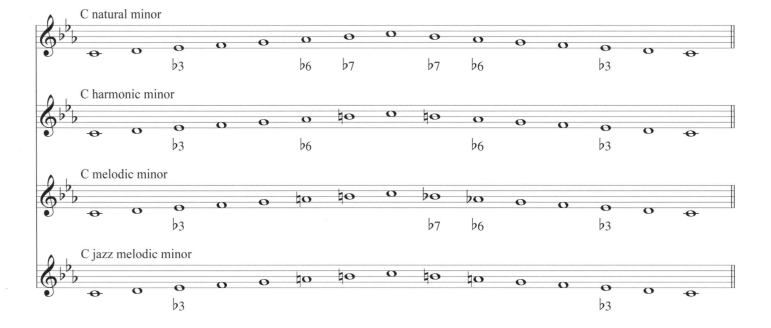

CHECKPOINT 3
Scales and Keys

1. Work out the relative minor or major of each of the following keys:

   - A major
   - F major
   - D major
   - B♭ major

   - F♯ major
   - A♭ major
   - C minor
   - G♯ minor

   - E minor
   - C♯ minor
   - B♭ minor
   - E♭ minor

2. Identify the following key signatures as both major and minor keys:

   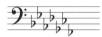

3. Spell out one octave of the following scales in text form:
   (Example: D major = D–E–F♯–G–A–B–C♯–D.)

   - B♭ major
   - F major
   - A major
   - A♭ major
   - B major
   - G♭ major

   - C natural minor
   - G♯ natural minor
   - A harmonic minor
   - C harmonic minor
   - F♯ harmonic minor

   - C♯ melodic minor (ascending and descending)
   - G melodic minor (ascending and descending)
   - F melodic minor (ascending and descending)

4. Write out the following scales on the stave using key signatures and accidentals where applicable:
   (Example: D melodic minor, ascending and descending.)

   - F harmonic minor - treble clef
   - E melodic minor - treble clef
   - C melodic minor - treble clef
   - B♭ melodic minor - treble clef
   - C♯ harmonic minor - treble clef

   - B melodic minor - bass clef
   - E♭ major - bass clef
   - G♭ major - bass clef
   - A melodic minor - bass clef
   - F♯ melodic minor - bass clef

5. Write out the following scales on the stave *without* the use of a key signature:
   (Example: E melodic minor.)

- F# harmonic minor - treble clef
- Bb melodic minor - bass clef
- Eb melodic minor - treble clef
- E major - bass clef
- C# major - treble clef

- G harmonic minor - bass clef
- B melodic minor - treble clef
- A major - bass clef
- Db major - treble clef
- F melodic minor - bass clef

6. Assuming the key signatures below represent major keys, identify the key and name the note (by name, scale step, and number) for each of the following examples:

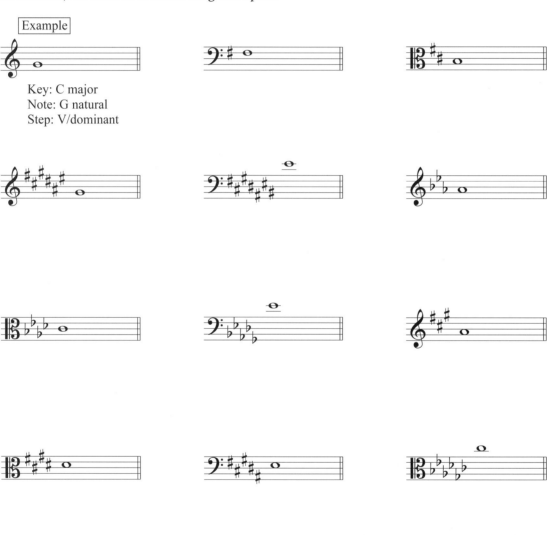

Key: C major
Note: G natural
Step: V/dominant

CHAPTER 5
Intervals

Any two notes can be defined in terms of the vertical space between them: how far apart they are. This measurement is called an *interval*.

The simplest form of interval measurement involves counting all the letter names involved in getting from one note to the other. The note C and the E directly above it comprise an interval of a third (C–D–E), E to A is a fourth (E–F–G–A), D to the C above is a seventh (D–E–F–G–A–B–C), and so on.

TRACK 23

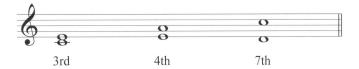

The interval designations here would be the same even if sharps and flats were introduced. C to E♭ is still a third of some kind, E♭ to A is also some type of fourth, and D to C♯ is a seventh, but clearly these intervals are different to those in the stave above. Intervals described in terms of number only are known as *generic intervals*. To define an interval more precisely, we have to count the number of half steps as well as the number of letter names. This further classification introduces the terms major, minor, perfect, diminished, and augmented.

The intervals from seconds to sevenths can be further classified as the following specific intervals (all are shown with C natural as the lower note for ease of comparison):

Seconds

TRACK 24

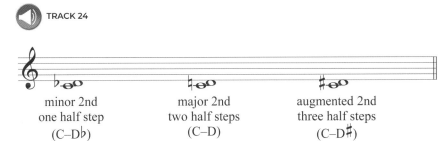

Thirds

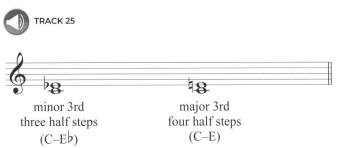
TRACK 25

Fourths

TRACK 26

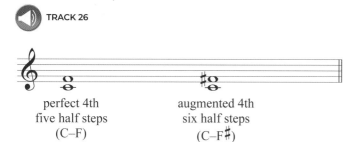

perfect 4th
five half steps
(C–F)

augmented 4th
six half steps
(C–F♯)

Fifths

TRACK 27

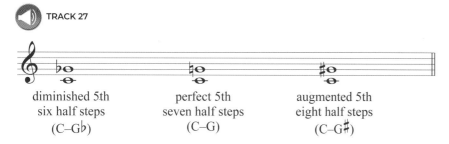

diminished 5th
six half steps
(C–G♭)

perfect 5th
seven half steps
(C–G)

augmented 5th
eight half steps
(C–G♯)

Sixths

TRACK 28

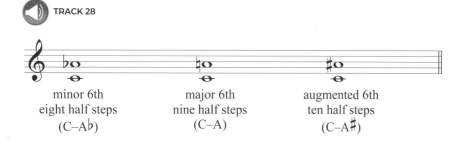

minor 6th
eight half steps
(C–A♭)

major 6th
nine half steps
(C–A)

augmented 6th
ten half steps
(C–A♯)

Sevenths

TRACK 29

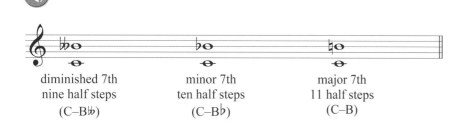

diminished 7th
nine half steps
(C–B♭♭)

minor 7th
ten half steps
(C–B♭)

major 7th
11 half steps
(C–B)

Notes

- Only fourths, fifths, and octaves may be designated perfect. There is no such thing as a perfect second, third, sixth, or seventh.

- Different intervals comprising enharmonically equivalent notes are also enharmonically equivalent. For example, F♯ and G♭ are enharmonically equivalent, so therefore are the intervals C–F♯ (augmented fourth) and C–G♭ (diminished fifth). In most situations, only one of the alternatives would be theoretically correct or applicable to the musical context.

- Some intervals are theoretically possible but rarely encountered to describe real-world combinations. For example, C–E♯ would have to be labelled an augmented third, while C–F♭ would be a diminished fourth.

Compound Intervals

Intervals larger than an octave, called *compound intervals*, are described using numbers above eight, and follow exactly the same logic as intervals within the octave. For example, C to D in the next octave is a major ninth. To find the corresponding simple interval from a compound interval, simply subtract seven. Some examples are shown below.

 TRACK 30

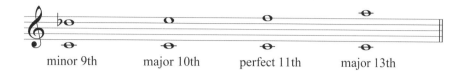

minor 9th   major 10th   perfect 11th   major 13th

Complementary Intervals

As we have seen, two notes an octave apart have the same pitch class and in many ways sound like the same note. It follows that transposing the lower note of any interval up by an octave, or the upper note down, will result in a different interval that sounds very similar. These are called *complementary intervals*, or *interval inversions*. For example, the interval C–G is a perfect fifth. Transposing the C up by one octave results in a perfect fourth (G–C). Therefore, the perfect fourth and perfect fifth are considered complementary intervals.

To find the correct name of the inversion of any known interval:

- First subtract the first interval's number from nine. This gives the following complementary generic intervals:
  › second: seventh
  › third: sixth
  › fourth: fifth
  › fifth: fourth
  › sixth: third
  › seventh: second

- Next, apply the following correspondences between an original specific interval and its inversion:
  › perfect: perfect
  › major: minor
  › minor: major
  › augmented: diminished
  › diminished: augmented

Examples:
- major second : minor seventh
- major third : minor sixth
- augmented fourth: diminished fifth
- augmented second : diminished seventh
- major seventh : minor second

Consonance and Dissonance

There is a spectrum of intervals from those considered the most consonant to those considered the most dissonant. In practice, this effect depends heavily on context and musical style. While dissonance can be an end in itself, and an integral part of some styles, in other styles, it must be handled carefully.

As interval inversions are considered equally consonant or dissonant, they may be classified together. The spectrum from most consonant to most dissonant runs as follows (some enharmonically equivalent intervals are omitted here as they sound the same):

- Octave (most consonant)
- Perfect fifth/Perfect fourth
- Major third/Minor sixth
- Major second/Minor seventh
- Minor second/Major seventh
- Augmented fourth/Diminished fifth (most dissonant)

Note that the augmented fourth and diminished fifth are complementary intervals and also enharmonically equivalent. In either inversion, the interval may also be called a *tritone*, as it spans three whole tones. The tritone plays a fundamental role in jazz harmony (see Chapter 13). Up to the Renaissance it was considered so ugly as to often be called *diabolus in musica* ("the devil in music"). Beyond the octave, the minor ninth is generally considered even more dissonant than the tritone.

(see Chapter 13)

TOOLBOX

Recognizing Intervals

One way to internalize the sounds of musical intervals is to associate them with the opening notes of familiar pieces of music. The following are suggested as a starting point:

Octave	Judy Garland: "Somewhere Over the Rainbow" ("Some - where")
Major Seventh	A-ha: "Take On Me" ("Take - on") Norah Jones: "Don't Know Why" ("I - waited")
Minor Seventh:	"Somewhere" (from *West Side Story*) ("There's a...")
Major Sixth:	Duke Ellington: "Take the 'A' Train"
Minor Sixth:	The Beatles: "In My Life" (intro)
Perfect Fifth:	"Baa Baa Black Sheep" ("Baa baa - black sheep")
Perfect Fourth:	"Auld Lang Syne" ("Should old")
Major Third:	The Beatles: "Can't Buy Me Love" ("Can't buy")
Minor Third:	Deep Purple: "Smoke on the Water" (intro) Katy Perry: "Firework" ("Do you")
Major Second:	"Do, Re, Mi" (from *The Sound of Music*) ("Do, Re")
Minor Second:	Theme from *Jaws*

Parallel Lines: The Building Blocks of Harmony

In many contexts and styles, the notes of a melody or other musical line may be supplemented by adding a second line that maintains a fixed (usually consonant) interval above or below it to create a simple form of harmony. In order to stay within the key, this means that the specific intervals used will vary. For example, parallel thirds in a major key may be either major or minor depending on the scale step. Harmonizing the major scale in thirds gives rise to the following specific intervals:

 TRACK 31

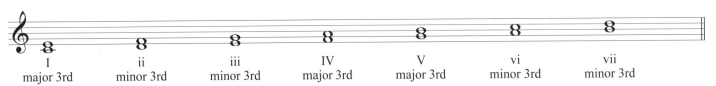

These are known as *diatonic thirds*, meaning that they belong to a key and therefore differ in internal composition. Different parallel intervals have very distinct sounds. Knowledge of these flavors is extremely useful to all musicians; composers, arrangers, orchestrators, instrumentalists, and backing vocalists often access radically different sonic flavors by deciding which parallel intervals to use.

Thirds

Thirds are perhaps the easiest parallel intervals to apply in many styles, and many singers use them intuitively when harmonizing. Harmony vocals in parallel thirds can be found across much of popular music, and play a large part in the style of vocal duos including the Everly Brothers, the Righteous Brothers, and Simon & Garfunkel.

YOU'VE LOST THAT LOVING FEELING
Words and Music by BARRY MANN, CYNTHIA WEIL and PHIL SPECTOR

Instrumental thirds sound equally distinctive and are often used on the guitar using the technique known as *double stopping* (simply put: playing two notes at once).

BROWN EYED GIRL
Words and Music by VAN MORRISON

This intro, which is arguably as much of a "hook" as the vocal line, uses double-stopped lead guitar thirds. Even without the bass and rhythm guitar parts, this would be a self-contained way to outline the harmony of the song.

Fourths and Fifths

Parallel fourths and fifths occur much less frequently than thirds in both classical and popular music. Traditional classical harmony (see Chapter 11) teaches that they should be avoided altogether except in a few very specific circumstances, and certainly not used for an entire phrase or line. This is partly because they have a slightly primitive, medieval quality; in fact, they were commonplace in medieval plainchant (church singing).

This earthy flavor, and the fact that they are less easy to find intuitively, has made fourths and fifths relatively rare in pop, but when they occur they are very distinctive and instantly recognizable.

EIGHT DAYS A WEEK
Words and Music by JOHN LENNON and PAUL McCARTNEY

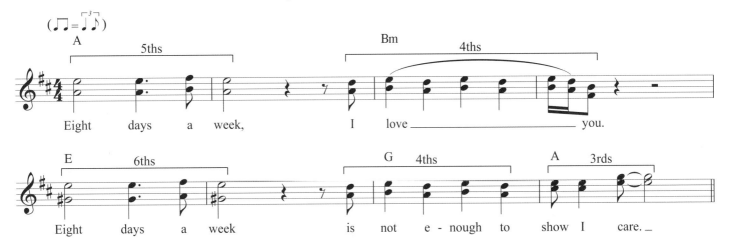

The bridge section of this early Beatles classic has a very distinctive sound as a result of its use of parallel fourths and fifths between Lennon and McCartney's voices. Only the end of the final phrase reverts to the more commonplace use of thirds, signaling a return to the mood of the verse and chorus.

Sixths

As sixths and thirds are complementary intervals, their use is in many ways interchangeable. However, as thirds are the narrowest consonant interval, they may sound a little too sweet or twee in many situations. This effect can be reduced by using sixths. They also often occur naturally when a male vocalist harmonizes behind a female lead, as a sixth below will generally sit more comfortably in the male range than a third above.

EVERYTHING HAS CHANGED
Words and Music by TAYLOR SWIFT and ED SHEERAN

This is a perfect example of female and male vocals in sixths (the last note of each phrase is a fifth, as this fits with the prevailing harmony).

Sevenths

The previous examples have all used consonant intervals. Dissonant harmonization can be used creatively too. Seconds sound *very* scrunchy (listen to almost any solo by jazz pianist Thelonious Monk for examples). This effect can be tempered by using sevenths (the complementary interval) instead. The result is ambiguous, spacey, and modern without being quite as strident.

FOR GOOD
(from the Broadway Musical *Wicked*)
Music and Lyrics by STEPHEN SCHWARTZ

The sevenths here are the perfect choice to evoke the desired other-worldly atmosphere of the story, while staying within a definite key.

CHAPTER 6
Triads and the Harmonized Major Scale

When two or more notes are sounded together, the result is called a *chord*. A chord may have any number of notes. The most fundamental type of chord in Western music, forming the basis on which more complex harmony can be built, is the three-note chord, or *triad*.

Conventionally, the three notes of a triad are separated by thirds. A triad can be constructed from any root note by adding a note a third above, and another a third above that. Because this produces an interval of a fifth between the outer notes, the three notes of a triad are known as the root, third, and fifth.

The major scale can be harmonized by taking each successive note as the root note of a triad and adding a third and fifth to each using diatonic notes (notes available in the key).

TRACK 37

Notice that these triads do not all sound the same. This is because the specific intervals within each triad vary. In chords I, IV, and V, the third is major while in all the others it is minor. The fifth in chord vii is a diminished fifth from the root, while in all the others it is a perfect fifth.

As there are two types of diatonic third interval (major and minor) and a triad is two thirds stacked together, there are four potential types of triad: major, minor, diminished, and augmented.

The augmented triad does not occur in the harmonized major scale. Major, minor, and diminished triads occur as follows:

TRACK 38

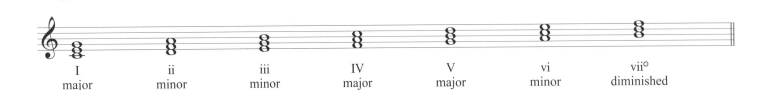

In classical harmony, the harmonic minor scale is used to generate minor key harmony. Minor, major, diminished, and augmented triads occur in this scale as follows:

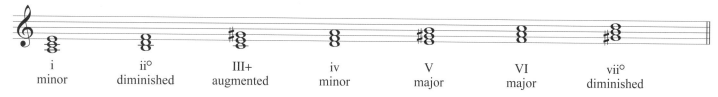

By convention, when Roman numerals are used to denote triads or other chords. they are usually capitalized for major chords and written in lowercase for minor or diminished chords. In major keys, this also reflects the fact that chords I, IV, and V are considered the primary (most important) chords.[12]

For the sake of clarity and familiarity with the individual sounds of the various triad types, it is useful to compare the construction and sound of the four triad types from the same root.

Primary and Secondary Triads: Major Key

The various triads in a major or minor key can be considered as having different roles within the key. Normally, the triads built on steps I, IV, and V are considered to be the most important in the key. For this reason, they are called *primary* triads.

In a major key, the primary chords are the three major chords in the key, perhaps another reason why they sound more significant and strong than the other chords.

Taking C major as an example, the three primary triads are C major (I/tonic), F major (IV/subdominant), and G major (V/dominant).

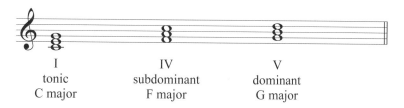

The other triads in the major key are known as *secondary* or *auxiliary chords*.

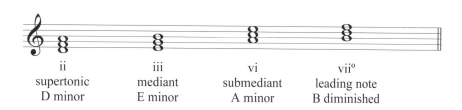

---

12   There is considerable variation in this practice.

Because they share some notes with the primary chords, they can also be used as substitutes for the primary chords when a different sound is required. These shared notes overlap (for example, chord iii has notes in common with both I and V, but the most important relationships are shown below, again in C major for reference).

TRACK 46

Primary Triads: Minor Key

In a minor key, the primary triads are also chords i, iv, and v. Using the harmonic minor scale as the source for these results in minor triads on i and iv, but a major triad (because in contains the raised leading note) for chord V. These are shown below in the key of A minor.

TRACK 47

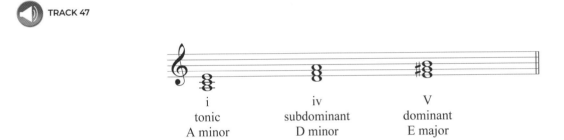

The secondary chords in the minor key are a little more complicated. Chord VI is a major chord and has two notes in common with chord i. In the harmonic minor, chords ii and vii are diminished, and both have notes in common with chord V. Chord III may be either major (drawing from the natural minor) or augmented (from the harmonic minor).

TRACK 48

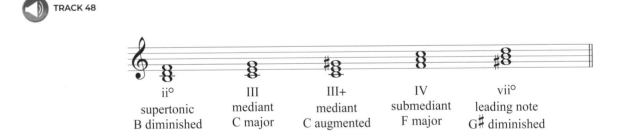

The augmented chord III is rarely used in classical or pop harmony. The major chord III is used freely in pop music. In classical music, it tends to be used carefully to avoid creating confusion, as it can also be heard as chord I of the related major key.

Primary Triads in All Keys

Instant recall of the notes of primary triads in both major and minor keys is an important part of a developing understanding of harmony and music theory in general. Here they are for reference.

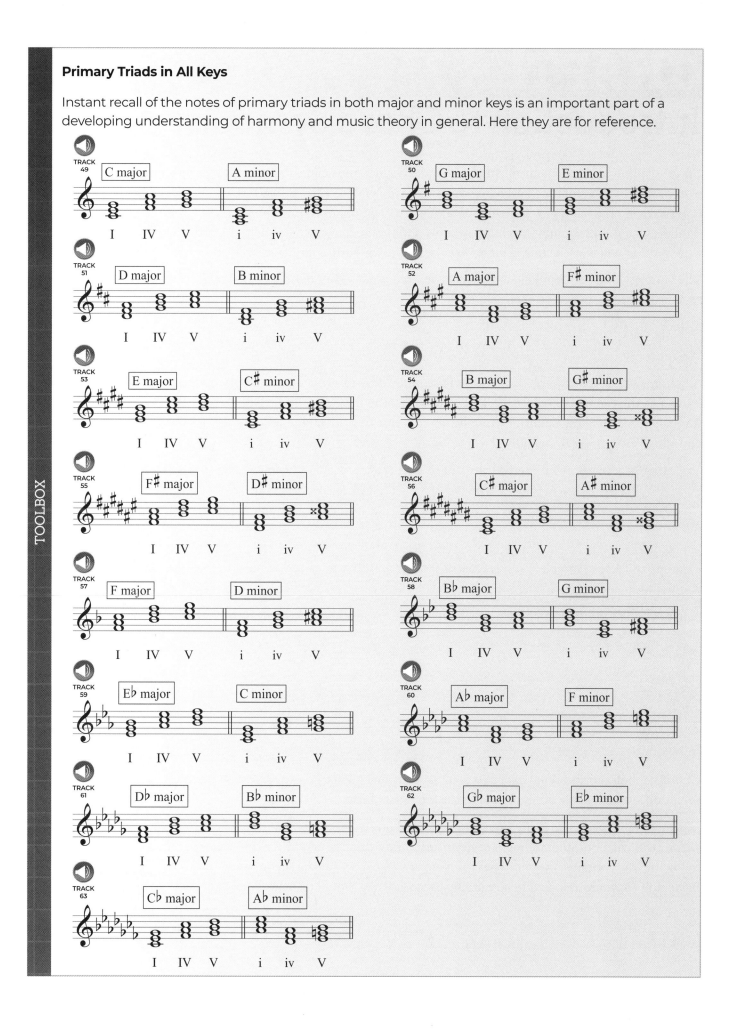

CHAPTER 7
Introduction to Chord Symbols

Chord symbols provide a convenient shorthand that gives musicians the information they need to construct their own parts. On the guitar or keyboard, reading chord symbols can often be easier than reading all the individual notes at once, and allows for more freedom of interpretation. In jazz, monophonic instruments also rely on chord symbols when improvising; the chord symbols outline the harmony and help the player choose notes, scales, and patterns that will work. Chord symbols are also useful for harmonic analysis.

The simplest form of chord symbol is a single note name. This signifies a major chord (triad) built on the note specified.

C   F#   E♭

(C major)   (F# major)   (E♭ major)

All chords other than simple major chords require some information to be placed after the note name. This is known as the *chord quality*, or *type*, and contains all the necessary information about the type of chord required (though some symbols denoting complex chords can be a little ambiguous, leaving room for discretion when choosing which notes to include).

The other triad types encountered thus far are usually shown using the lower case suffixes *m*, *dim*, and *aug*.

Cm   F#°   E♭+

(C minor)   (F# diminished)   (E♭ augmented)

Unlike notes on the stave, key signatures and accidentals do not affect chord symbols. Even if the key signature contains an F#, for example, F always means F natural. If F# is intended, it must be written.

Chord symbols are usually placed above the stave. Whereas the stave contains the melody, the two combined can convey enough information for a whole band. This format is known as *top line* or *lead sheet* format.

TRACK 64

Chord symbols are also often added to pop piano arrangements, both to give pianists more freedom in their interpretation, and to enable other players to use the same music.

Jazz musicians (particularly rhythm section players) often use charts that omit the melody, placing chord symbols within the bar lines and adding any necessary information about their rhythmic placement. For example, the following line contains one chord per measure of 4/4, except for the second measure where there are two chords. By default these are assumed to be equally spaced, so they should be placed on beats 1 and 3.

$\frac{4}{4}$ G7 | Gm7   C7♭9 | Am7 | D7♭9   ‖

(The chord symbols above specify more complex chords, some of which will be discussed later.)

When chord changes are intended to occur at precise points determined by more complex rhythms, these may be shown in addition, usually using *rhythm slashes*. These are written rhythms using a diagonal slash in place of the notehead, indicating that only the rhythm is specified.

Alternative Names

Minor: Cm; Cmin; C- (minus symbol)
(Applies also to more complex chords with a minor third, e.g. C-7, Cmin13, etc.)

Major 7: Cmaj7; CΔ7; CΔ
(The triangle denotes a major seventh interval, and also applies to more complex chords, e.g. CΔ9)

Diminished: Cdim; C°

Diminished 7: Cdim7; C°7

Half Diminished: Cm7♭5; Cø

Augmented: Caug; C+
(The + symbol denotes an augmented fifth from the root and can also give rise to other names such as C+7 for C7♯5.)

CHECKPOINT 4
Intervals, Triads, and Chord Symbols

The following exercises may be useful on a purely theoretical level, but a far greater benefit will be felt by also finding and playing each interval on a keyboard instrument.

1. Identify the following specific intervals in the key of C major:

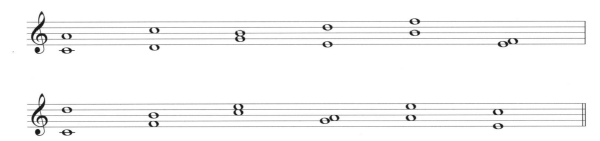

2. Identify the following specific intervals in B minor:

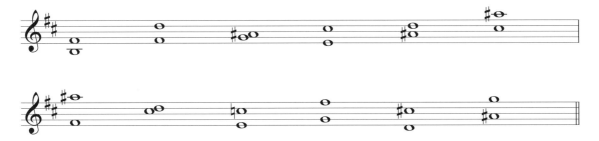

3. Add the following specific intervals above each note (no key signature; use accidentals where required):

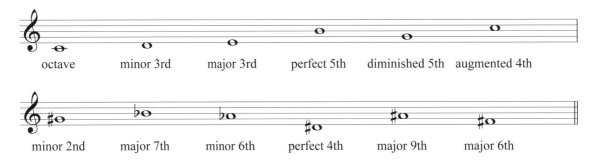

octave   minor 3rd   major 3rd   perfect 5th   diminished 5th   augmented 4th

minor 2nd   major 7th   minor 6th   perfect 4th   major 9th   major 6th

4. Add the following specific intervals below each note (no key signature; use accidentals where required):

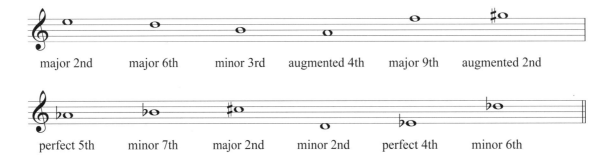

major 2nd   major 6th   minor 3rd   augmented 4th   major 9th   augmented 2nd

perfect 5th   minor 7th   major 2nd   minor 2nd   perfect 4th   minor 6th

5. Identify the following diatonic triads in F major, using both chord symbol and Roman numeral notation:

6. Identify the following diatonic triads in F# minor, using both chord symbol and Roman numeral notation:

7. Identify the following chords using chord symbols only (no key signature; accidentals only affect individual chords):

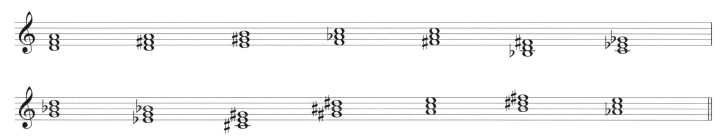

8. Add the missing thirds and fifths to the following root notes to complete the chords specified by the chord symbols (no key signature; use accidentals where required):

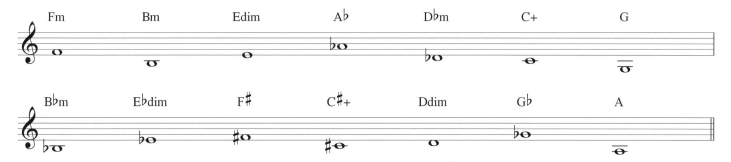

9. For each key signature shown on the following pages:
   - Identify both the major and relative minor key indicated.
   - Write out and label the primary chords (I, IV, and V) in the major key using Roman numerals and chord symbols.
   - Write out and label the primary chords (i, iv, and V) in the minor key using Roman numerals and chord symbols.

Example:

Exercises:

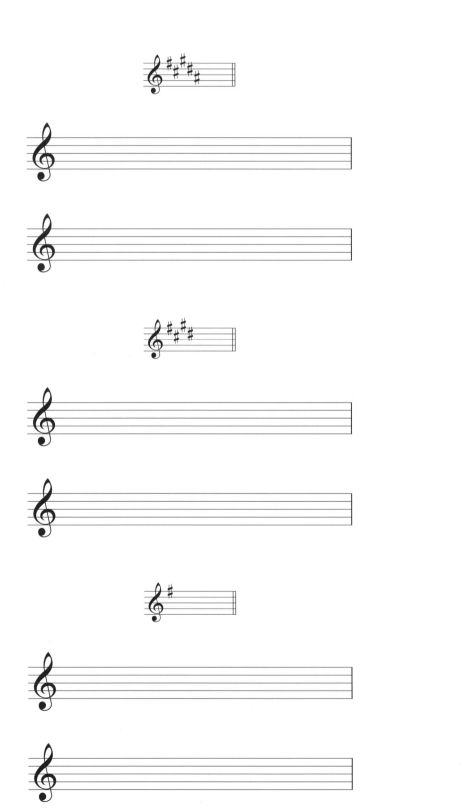

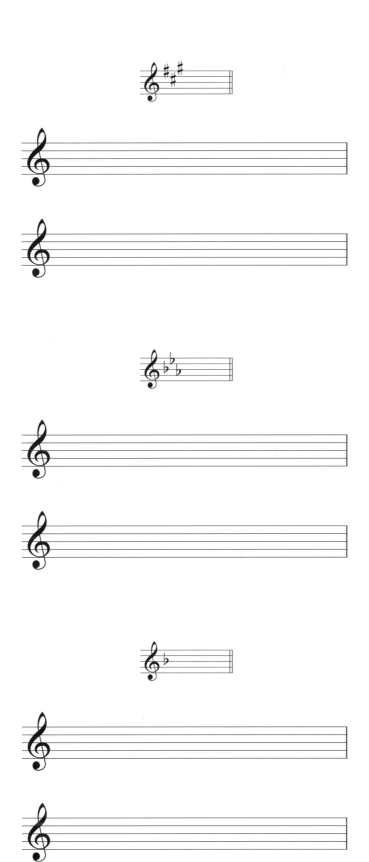

CHAPTER 8
Inversions

Triads and more complex chords do not always have to be arranged so that the root note is the lowest pitch. A chord with anything other than the root note as the lowest is called an *inversion*. A triad can therefore appear in three different guises: root position, first inversion (where the bass note is the third), and second inversion (where the bass note is the fifth). In this context, "bass note" simply means the lowest note played, whether or not it is in the register of a bass instrument or voice.

 TRACK 65

It follows that chords with more than three notes can have more inversions:

 TRACK 66

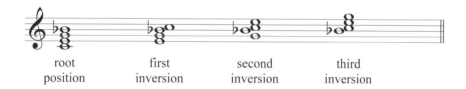

Terminology

In Roman numeral terminology, the scale degree may be followed by *a* to indicate root position, *b* for first inversion, *c* for second inversion, and so on. When only the numeral is shown, the chord is assumed to be in root position. The example below shows the tonic, supertonic, and mediant chords of G major labeled like this.

 TRACK 67

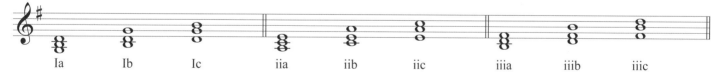

Chord Symbols

Inversions can be shown with chord symbols using a forward slash to separate the root and chord quality from the bass note, as in the examples below:

 TRACK 68

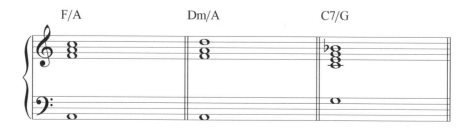

Slash symbols may be read in a few different ways: F/A may be read as "F over A," "F slash A," "F (major), first inversion," or "F with A in the bass."

Slashes may also be used to denote more complex chords, where the bass note would not otherwise be present in the chord, for example C/F and Em/A. Without the use of slashes, these chords would require more complex names.

Interval Analysis and Figured Bass

Inversions are sometimes labelled with reference to their internal intervals. Because a root position triad by definition has a fifth and a third above the bass note, it is sometimes called a "5/3" (five three) chord. In these terms, a first inversion is "6/3" and a second inversion is "6/4."

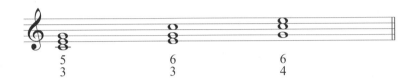

In Baroque music, a system known as *figured bass* expanded on this idea as a means of conveying harmony in the context of a bass line. In a Baroque orchestra or other ensemble, the harpsichordist could provide a fully realized harmonic accompaniment by reading the bass line part, which would be annotated using figured bass. In the example below, a bass note with no number represents a root position chord, "6" represents a first inversion, and other numbers represent more advanced harmony, including suspensions (see Chapter 9).

Inversions and Stepwise Bass Movement

Bass lines that move by step (using half or whole steps rather than larger intervals) are often highly effective, but harmonizing each bass note with a root position chord can sound musically clumsy. A more elegant solution is to use inversions in between root position chords. In classical harmony terms, this avoids the use of consecutive fifths and octaves (see Chapter 11).

TRACK 69

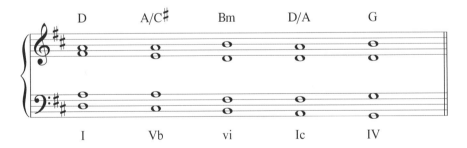

Inversions in Context

The verse chord sequence here uses inversions as passing chords to completely transform what would otherwise be an ordinary I–vi–IV–V sequence in E major (see Chapter 10): E and C#m are connected by B/D# (first inversion); C#m and A are connected by E/B (second inversion); finally, E/G# connects to a F#m (ii) before the bass changes to B to result in a dominant 11th chord (A/B—see Chapter 9 for more on this chord).

YOUR SMILING FACE
Words and Music by JAMES TAYLOR

TRACK
70

The bridge of this contemporary jazz classic also uses inversions as passing chords to great effect. Without them, the sequence would be a rather bland and un-jazzy I–ii–IV–vi. These are joined up using inversions which not only enable a gradually ascending bass line, but also introducing passing modulations via chromatic chords (see Chapter 12). Note also that root position chords coincide with the third in the melody while first inversions have the root in the melody. This way, the harmony remains balanced throughout.

JAMES
By PAT METHENY and LYLE MAYS

TRACK
71

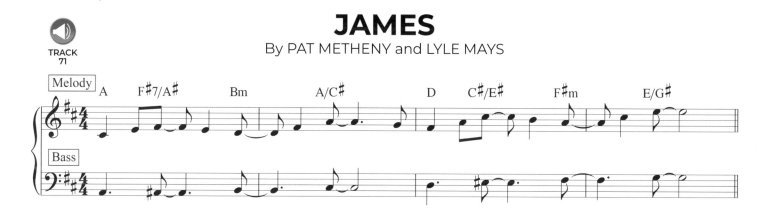

CHAPTER 9
Beyond Triads

While triads form the basis of conventional harmony, chords can be constructed using more notes, or by using intervals other than thirds. Chords of four notes and beyond form the basis of jazz harmony and much jazz-influenced pop; a triad in the middle of a jazz arrangement would often sound almost exotically plain.

Seventh Chords

Adding a third to a triad results in a chord known as a *seventh chord*, as the outer interval is a seventh.

Just as the two types of third result in four types of triads, there are, in theory, eight types of seventh chords based on stacked major and minor thirds, and still more if all types of fifth and seventh are allowed independently. The following diatonic seventh chords are commonly encountered within major and minor keys. For reference, the chord types detailed here are shown using the root notes A and C.

Chord "spellings" are often used to define the notes of a chord relative to the root. In this system, modern numerals are used, and relate to the steps major scale. In this sense, all seventh chords can be seen as modifications of the major seventh chord.

Major 7 (symbol: maj7)
Chord spelling: 1–3–5–7 (root, major third, perfect fifth, major seventh)

Dominant 7 (symbol: 7)
Chord spelling: 1–3–5–♭7 (root, major third, perfect fifth, minor seventh)

Minor 7 (symbol: m7)
Chord spelling: 1–♭3–5–♭7 (root, minor third, perfect fifth, minor seventh)

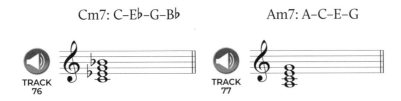

Minor 7 flat 5, also known as half diminished (symbol: m7♭5)

Chord spelling: 1–♭3–♭5–♭7 (root, minor third, diminished fifth, minor seventh)

Cm7(♭5): C–E♭–G♭–B♭   Am7(♭5): A–C–E♭–G

Diminished 7 (symbol: dim7)

Chord spelling: 1–♭3–♭5–♭♭7 (root, minor third, diminished fifth, diminished seventh)

Cdim7: C–E♭–G♭–B♭♭   Adim7: A–C–E♭–G♭

Minor (major 7) (symbol: m(maj7))

Chord spelling: 1–♭3–5–7 (root, minor third, perfect fifth, major seventh)

Cm(maj7): C–E♭–G–B   Am(maj7): A–C–E–G#

Sevenths as Diatonic Chords

Harmonizing the major scale using diatonic seventh chords results in the following chords on each step:

 TRACK 84

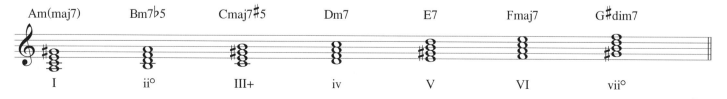

- Major seventh chords are found on steps I and IV.
- The dominant seventh is found only on V.
- Minor seventh chords are found on ii, ii, and vi.
- The half diminished chord is found only on step vii.

Harmonizing the harmonic minor scale using seventh chords results in the following on each step:

 TRACK 85

Am(maj7)	Bm7♭5	Cmaj7#5	Dm7	E7	Fmaj7	G#dim7
I	ii°	III+	iv	V	VI	vii°

In practice, some of these chords are not encountered very often, particularly the maj7(#5) chord.

The importance of the dominant seventh should be noted at this point. Of all the seventh chords in common use, it is the only one that unambiguously defines a key center. Whereas major seventh and minor seventh chords are found on several steps of the scale, the dominant seventh is found only on step V. In other words, when we encounter a maj7 or m7, we are not necessarily able to tell its function. A dominant seventh chord, on the other hand, can point to only one key center in conventional tonal harmony. However, because it appears as step V in both major and minor keys, it does not in itself define the tonality of the key center.

Beyond Sevenths

On a theoretical level, we can carry on adding thirds to generate five-, six-, and seven-note chords. Continuing the odd number pattern established (1–3–5–7), it follows that these chords would be known as ninth, 11th, and 13th chords. However, it becomes increasingly unlikely that all of the notes will actually be used. It is therefore also important to understand which notes are essential, and which may (or even, in some cases, must) be left out.

Just as there are more types of seventh chords than triads, there are more possible types of ninth, 11th, and 13th chords. However, many of these do not occur as diatonic chords. We will focus initially on the more frequently encountered chords.

Ninth Chords

In all common types of ninth chord, the fifth may often be omitted. The following are commonly encountered:

Major 9th (symbol: maj9)

Spelling: 1–3–(5)–7–9

Cmaj9: C–E–(G)–B–D   Amaj9: A–C#–(E)–G#–B

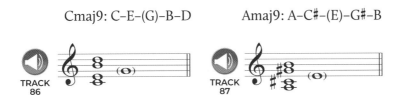

Dominant 9th (symbol: 9)

Spelling: 1–3–(5)–♭7–9

C9: C–E–(G)–B♭–D   A9: A–C#–(E)–G–B

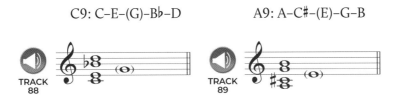

Minor 9th (symbol: m9)

Spelling: 1–♭3–(5)–♭7–9

Cm9: C–E♭–(G)–B♭–D   Am9: A–C–(E)–G–B

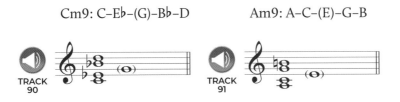

Eleventh Chords

Only two varieties of 11th chord are commonly encountered: the dominant 11th and the minor 11th.

Dominant 11th (symbol: 11)

As with all ninth chords, the fifth may or may not be present. The major third, if used, would create a dissonant minor 9th interval against the 11th. It is therefore omitted, enabling dominant 11th chords to function as *suspensions* (see below).

Spelling: 1–3–(5)–♭7–9–11

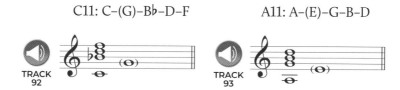

C11: C–(G)–B♭–D–F   A11: A–(E)–G–B–D

Notice that the essential notes other than the root make up a major triad in their own right. In other words, C11 can be viewed as a B♭ major triad with a C bass note, and A11 as a G major triad over an A. This results in the use of alternative chord symbols such as B♭/C and G/A (see Chapter 13 for more on these slash chord symbols).

Minor 11th (symbol: m11)

1–♭3–(5)–♭7–(9)–11

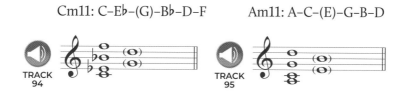

Cm11: C–E♭–(G)–B♭–D–F   Am11: A–C–(E)–G–B–D

Thirteenth Chords

Two diatonic 13th chords are commonly encountered: the major 13th and (more frequently) dominant 13th chords. In both cases, the potential clash between the major third and 11th is resolved by omitting the 11th.

Major 13th (symbol: maj13)

Spelling: 1–3–(5)–7–(9)–11–13

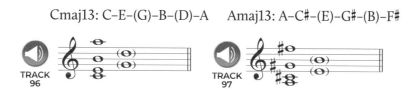

Cmaj13: C–E–(G)–B–(D)–A   Amaj13: A–C♯–(E)–G♯–(B)–F♯

Dominant 13th (symbol: 13)

Spelling: 1–3–(5)–♭7–(9)–11–13

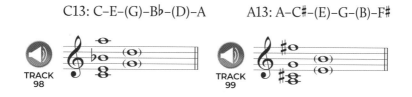

C13: C–E–(G)–B♭–(D)–A   A13: A–C♯–(E)–G–(B)–F♯

Non-Triadic Chords

Though stacking notes in thirds forms the basis of Western harmony, there are many departures from this norm. These include suspensions, chords with added notes, and *quartal* chords (built from fourths, rather than thirds).

Suspensions

The character of a major chord is defined by its third. If we substitute this for an adjacent note, the character of the chord becomes ambiguous; the adjacent note seems to "want" to resolve to the third. The adjacent note may be a half step above (a perfect fourth from the root) or a whole step below (a major second from the root). The resulting chords are the suspended fourth chord (symbol: sus4) and suspended second chord (symbol: sus2).

When a suspension is followed by the major chord to which it is related, this is called *resolution*. In classical harmony, in which many other types of suspension are also encountered, strict rules are generally observed (in particular that suspensions must always be resolved). In pop music, they are often used more freely. The example below shows sus2 and sus4 chords, with resolutions.

TRACK 100

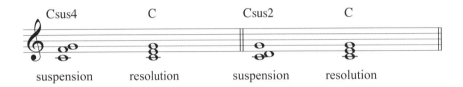

Added Notes

Various notes other than further thirds may be added to triads to create color. In popular music, these are generally shown with the symbol "add" followed by the interval added in relation to the root, except if this is a sixth; these are simply known as *sixth chords* (symbol: 6).

By convention, "add" chords usually specify the added note as a compound interval: nine instead of two, 11 instead of four, even if the added note is in the same octave as the root. There is no particularly logical reason for this other than perhaps to avoid confusion with suspensions. Add2 and add4 are also occasionally encountered.

The added ninth may be used to color both major and minor triads. Note that "add" also implies that there is no seventh. If there were, the chord would be some kind of 9 (not add9) chord.

The following example shows both major and minor added ninth chords.

TRACK 101

Add4 chords are less frequently encountered than add9 chords, but occasionally appear as a result of guitarists letting open strings ring against simple triad shapes. The sound is something of a clash (as the 11th/fourth above clashes with the major third) but has nonetheless become a distinctive guitar trick.

TRACK 102

Sixth Chords

The other note frequently added to both major and minor triads is the major sixth. Two chord types result: the major sixth (or just "sixth") chord (symbol: 6) and minor sixth (symbol: m6).

Major sixth chords are usually considered functionally equivalent to major triads and major seventh chords (in both chord I and chord IV, the major sixth note belongs in the key).

Major sixth chords are often encountered as final chords.

 TRACK 103

Quartal/Quintal Chords

The concept of stacking thirds is easy to adapt conceptually. What if we stacked notes separated by some other interval, such as fourths?

 TRACK 104

A stack of diatonic fourths, as seen here, results in a chord that is primarily usable in jazz and contemporary classical music. The stack of fifths in a tonic major context, however, produces a five-note chord containing a perfect fifth, major ninth, and compound versions of the major sixth and major third.

 TRACK 105

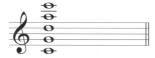

The resulting *six-nine* (symbol: 6/9) chord has a highly distinctive flavor. In many contexts (including guitar and piano), it is voiced by inverting the arrangement of all notes above the root so they become perfect fourths. The 6/9 chord may therefore be considered a quartal chord in this guise. Lowering the third results in a minor six-nine (symbol: m6/9) chord.

 TRACK 106

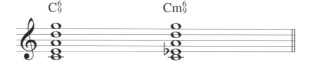

Power Chords

Rock music (and heavy rock in particular) often makes use of chords with fewer than three unique notes. These are generally known as *power chords* and consist only of the root note and perfect fifth. Sometimes, either or both notes are repeated in higher octaves.

Power chords are associated with the electric guitar, and often with the use of heavy distortion. Because a distorted guitar sound is so rich in harmonics, full major or minor chords often sound rather busy and congested, whereas the root and fifth can co-exist more easily along with their respective harmonics. Power chords are neither explicitly major nor minor, and can therefore be used in place of both. They are normally notated with the chord quality suffix "5."

> **Distinctive Chords in Context**
>
> Certain chords sound so distinctive that if we encounter them in a famous or particularly great piece of music, we are likely to continue to identify it with that piece, and we can easily call the sound to mind by mentally hearing the piece again.
>
> The following songs make particularly memorable use of particular chords and are therefore well worth listening to with this in mind. Some of these examples use arpeggiated or broken chords (where the notes of the chord are played sequentially rather than together). If anything, this makes the sound of the chord even easier to internalize.

This early 20th century piece makes very simple and effective use of repeated major seventh chords (chords IV and I in D major).

GYMNOPÉDIE NO. 1
(from *Three Gymnopédies*)
By ERIK SATIE

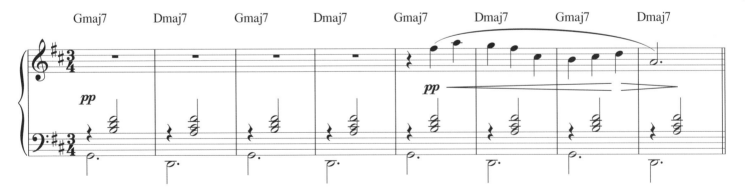

The intro to this song incorporates an arpeggiated Dsus4 chord. The suspension then resolves to a simple D chord.

TRACK
111

MORE THAN A FEELING
Words and Music by TOM SCHOLZ

The sound of the dominant ninth can be memorized in the form of the ensemble phrase (bass and horns) at the end of each chorus here, which ascends through the notes of a D9 chord.

TRACK
112

I GOT YOU (I FEEL GOOD)
Words and Music by JAMES BROWN

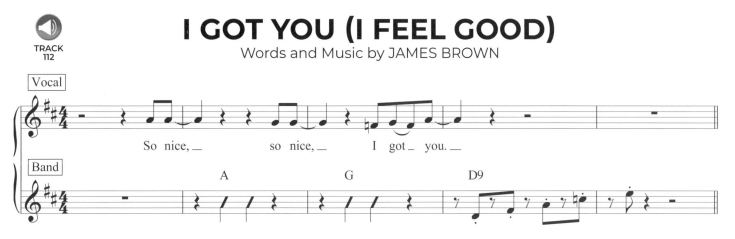

Eleventh chords are often written as slash chords. Either way, the sound is unmistakeable in its dramatic effect, where the piano here is joined by strings and brass after the first line of each verse.

TRACK
113

THE LONG AND WINDING ROAD
Words and Music by JOHN LENNON and PAUL McCARTNEY

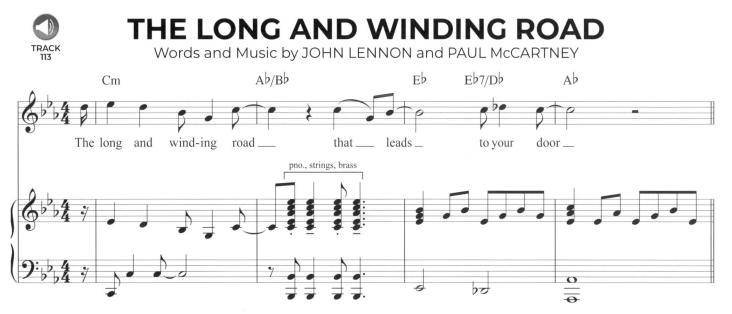

The open, ambiguous sound of the sus2 chord made it something of a favorite in 1980s pop. Although functioning as chords I and vi in the key of E♭ major here, the omission of the third makes all the difference.

TRACK 114

DON'T DREAM IT'S OVER
Words and Music by NEIL FINN

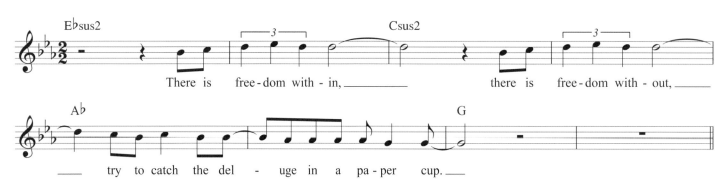

This intro and verse accompaniment pattern is the perfect distillation of the sound of add9 chords, functioning as chords I and vi in the major key. The subsequent sus2 chords are IV and V. This most basic chord progression (see Chapter 10) sounds so much more sophisticated as a result of these chords in place of major and minor triads.

TRACK 115

EVERY BREATH YOU TAKE
Music and Lyrics by STING

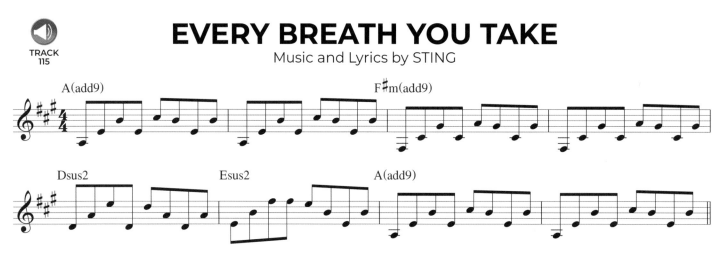

This intro riff embodies the sound of classic rock, using power chords throughout. On the guitar, these are inverted and voiced as perfect fourths, but the effect is the same.

TRACK 116

SMOKE ON THE WATER
Words and Music by RITCHIE BLACKMORE, IAN GILLAN,
ROGER GLOVER, JON LORD and IAN PAICE

CHECKPOINT 5
Beyond Triads and Inversions

All exercises here have no key signature. Accidentals affect only individual chords.

1. Construct the following chords in root position on the treble clef from the root and quality given:

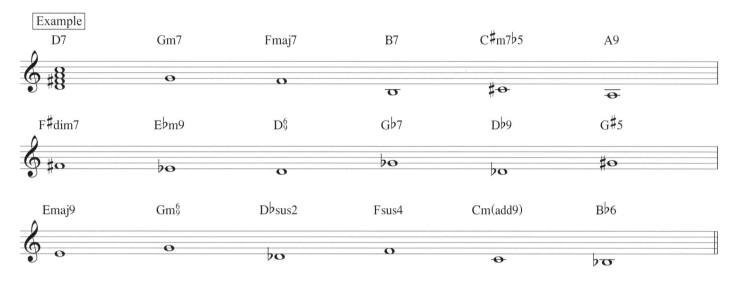

2. Construct the following chords with the root note in the bass clef and all the other notes in the treble clef:

3. Identify the following root position chords in treble clef:

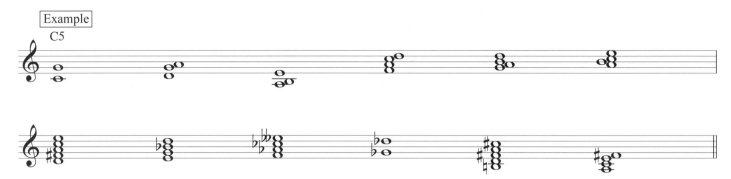

4. Name the following inversions using slash notation. The chord root and quality are defined by the notes in the treble clef (not necessarily in root position), while the bass clef defines the bass note (after the slash):

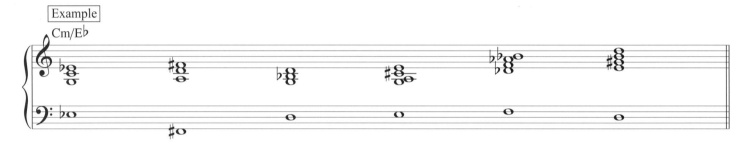

5. Name the following inversions using slash notation. The chord root and quality are defined by the notes in both clefs (so the bass note is not necessarily doubled in the treble clef), while the bass clef defines the bass note (after the slash):

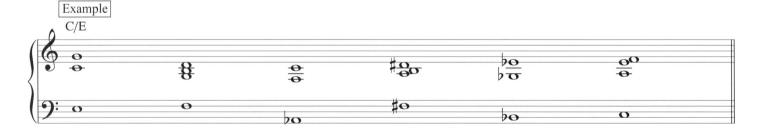

CHAPTER 10
Chord Sequences

One of the defining features of a piece of music—particularly in any popular music style—is its chord sequence. Many songs are constructed using a repetitive chord sequence throughout, while others use several sequences to distinguish different parts of the song. This chapter will examine some of the most important sequences.

I–vi–IV–V

This sequence is strongly associated with American pop of the 1950s, and is often called the *'50s progression* or *doo-wop progression*, though its most famous use actually dates from 1961: Ben E. King's "Stand by Me." Here, the bass part outlines the repeated chord sequence throughout, and the root movement is often doubled by strings. Familiarity with this song should enable easy identification of this chord sequence whenever it is encountered.

TRACK
117

STAND BY ME
Words and Music by JERRY LEIBER, MIKE STOLLER and BEN E. KING

Listening:

Other songs built wholly or partly around the "Stand by Me" sequence include:
- "Perfect" (Ed Sheeran)
- "A Teenager in Love" (Dion & The Belmonts)
- "(What a) Wonderful World" (Sam Cooke)
- "Eternal Flame" (The Bangles)
- "I Will Always Love You" (Dolly Parton/Whitney Houston)
- "Octopus's Garden" (The Beatles)

I–vi–ii–V

There are many variations of the above sequence. One possibility is to substitute chord ii for chord IV. Variations on the I–vi–ii–V sequence abound in jazz (most notably, Gershwin's "I Got Rhythm," which forms the basis for many jazz standards). It is perhaps a more satisfactory progression than I–vi–IV–V as it can be seen as a partial cycle of fifths (see next page) from chord vi with its final resolution on chord I. One of the most famous songs built mainly around this sequence is "The Wonder of You" (most famously recorded by Elvis Presley).

THE WONDER OF YOU
Words and Music by BAKER KNIGHT

Listening:

Other songs built around this sequence include:

- "This Boy" (The Beatles)
- "Heart and Soul" (Hoagy Carmichael)
- "Fluorescent Adolescent" (Arctic Monkeys)
- "Beauty School Dropout" (from *Grease*)
- "Hungry Heart" (Bruce Springsteen)
- "Blue Moon" (Billie Holiday)

I–V–vi–IV

The chords of the "Stand by Me" sequence can be rearranged to give I–V–vi–IV—a prevalent progression in pop music from the 1970s onwards, and often associated with songs with an "anthemic" quality. The sequence also often appears in slightly modified form (starting at a different point), for example as vi–IV–I–V.

WITH OR WITHOUT YOU
Words and Music by U2

Listening:

Other songs built around this sequence include:

- "Torn" (Natalie Imbruglia)
- "Don't Stop Believin'" (Journey)
- "I'm Yours" (Jason Mraz)
- "Fall at Your Feet (Crowded House)"
- "You're Beautiful" [verse] (James Blunt)
- "Someone You Loved" (Lewis Capaldi)

Cyclical Progressions

The cycle or circle of fifths concept turns up in many places in music theory (see Chapter 4) and translates into a highly effective way to construct a chord sequence. Chords tend to want to resolve down a fifth (or up a fourth). A chain of these resolutions works because, while each resolution is satisfactory, the full cycle represents a longer journey with its own resolution. This type of chord sequence has roots deep in the history of classical music, and was often used by Baroque composers including Corelli, Handel, and Bach. In the 20th century, it became a common device and found its way into many standard songs in musical theatre and jazz.

TRACK
120

AUTUMN LEAVES

English lyric by JOHNNY MERCER · French lyric by JACQUES PREVERT
Music by JOSEPH KOSMA

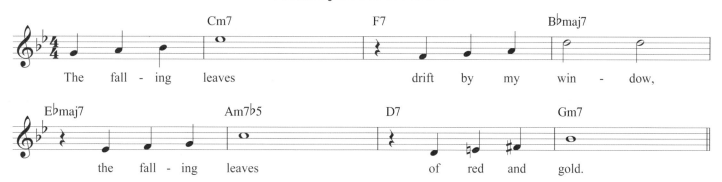

The cyclical progression in this jazz standard can be viewed as being in G minor throughout, or alternatively as modulating between B♭ major and G minor (see Chapter 12 for more on modulation). Notice also that all chords here are sevenths. This is idiomatic to jazz in general but also to any cyclical progression as the seventh of each chord either resolves to (or becomes) the third of the next chord:

TRACK 121

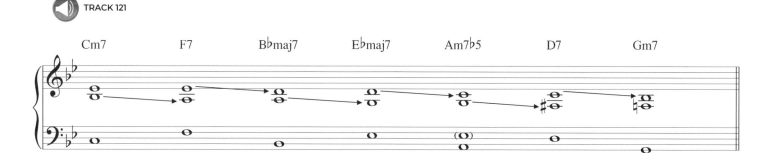

Notice also that this type of progression lends itself to melodies where, as above, a phrase is transposed to create a melodic sequence (see Glossary).

Listening:

Other songs which make use of the full or partial cyclical progressions include:

- "Love You Like a Love Song" (Selena Gomez & The Scene)
- "Fly Me to the Moon" (Bart Howard)
- "All the Things You Are" (Jerome Kern)
- "Parisienne Walkways" (Gary Moore & Phil Lynott)
- "I Will Survive" (Gloria Gaynor)

12-Bar Blues

This sequence is central to the development of the blues and all styles that flowed from it, including jazz and rock 'n' roll.

In its basic form, the early 12-bar sequence usually used just the three primary chords of the major key. Originating in the field hollers and spirituals of African American slaves, and later, freedmen, the dissonances in early blues that soon became characterized as *blue notes* arose through the combination of these chords with the minor pentatonic scale. In particular, the minor third and minor seventh of the minor pentatonic resulted in clashes against the tonic and dominant chords. Later, these notes began to be assimilated into the harmony, resulting in a somewhat standardized 12-bar form using dominant seventh-type chords throughout.

$\frac{4}{4}$ G7 | G7 | G7 | G7 . |

C7 | C7 | G7 | G7 |

D7 | C7 | G7 | D7   ‖

A practically infinite number of variations on this chord structure are possible, particularly in jazz where the sequence tends to be embellished using ii–V progressions (see Chapter 13). One of the most common variations, found in blues and rock as well as jazz, is the use of chord IV in the second measure, as seen on the next page in Lowell Fulson's "Reconsider Baby."

> "Reconsider Baby" appears on the next page to allow for easier reading.

RECONSIDER BABY
Words and Music by LOWELL FULSON

So long, _____ oh, I hate _ to see you go. So long, _ _____ oh, I hate _ to see you go. And the way _ ___ that I will miss you, I ___ guess you will nev - er know.

Listening:

Other songs based on the 12-bar blues progression include:

- "Johnny B. Goode" (Chuck Berry)
- "Sweet Home Chicago" (Robert Johnson/Blues Brothers)
- "Blues Before Sunrise" (Leroy Carr/Eric Clapton)
- "Blue Suede Shoes" (Carl Perkins/Elvis Presley)
- "Blue Monk" (Thelonious Monk)
- "Twisted" (Annie Ross/Joni Mitchell)

TOOLBOX

More Sequences

The following sequences are also frequently encountered. Some of them may be viewed as variants of the sequences above. All of these are excellent starting points for generating new chord sequences.

Sequence	Example in C major
I–iii–IV–V	C–Em–F–G
I–V–vi–iii–IV–I–(ii)–V	C–G–Am–Em–F–C–(Dm)–G ("Pachelbel's Canon," Green Day's "Basket Case")
I7–V7–I7–IV7	C7–G7–C7–F7
I7–V7–I7–V7	C7–G7–C7–G7 (Eight-Bar Blues)
I–I–I–I	C–C–C–C
I–I–V7–V7	C–C–G7–G7
I–I7–IV–IV*	C–C7–F–F
I–V7–I–I	C–G7–C–C ("When the Saints Go Marching In")

* The second IV chord is often minor—see Chapter 12.

CHAPTER 11
Introduction to Classical Harmony

The study of classical harmony can provide a useful grounding for musicians of any style and background. Even though many of its rules most closely reflect the practices of 18th century composers such as Bach and Handel, and do not always apply to pop, rock, and jazz, the guiding principles and frame of reference are important to a developing understanding of all musical styles.

The traditional system of classical harmony may be used as a basis for writing for any combination of instruments or voices. However, the fundamentals of harmony are considered in terms of four parts, reflecting the main designations of adult singing voices: *soprano*, *alto*, *tenor*, and *bass* (abbreviated to SATB).

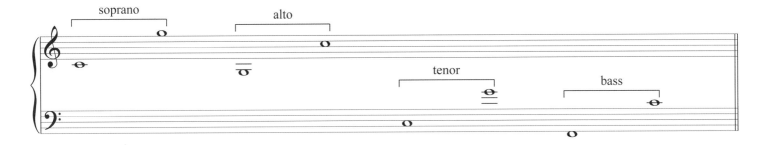

For the purposes of study and analysis, the four voices are usually written as a short score on the treble and bass clefs with S and A in treble clef and T and B in the bass clef. S and T stems are written upwards while A and B are written downwards. The soprano part is often termed the melody, though melodic writing can occur in any part.

TRACK 123

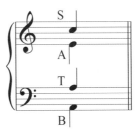

This is easier to manage and analyze than four separate staves, yet still allows for rhythmic independence between parts. The example below shows some eighth-note movement in the melody, while other parts proceed in quarter notes.

TRACK 124

The study of classical harmony in this form usually begins by establishing certain strict rules. The most important of these are:

- Any four notes that sound together are considered as a chord. The notes of any chord are distributed between the parts S, A, T, and B, observing the permitted range for each part.

- Classical harmony is mainly based on triads. To produce four-part harmony, one note in any triad must be used twice, or doubled. The general order of preference when deciding which note to double is root, fifth, third. The third of a minor chord may be doubled but the third of a major chord should not usually be doubled.

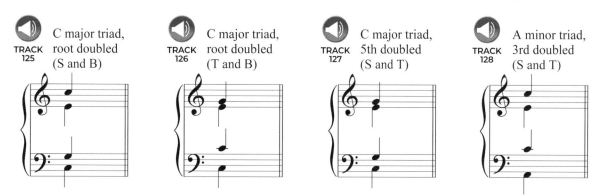

- The fifth of a chord may sometimes be omitted, but the third may not (as this determines the quality of the chord).

- Adjacent parts should not be more than an octave apart, except for the tenor and bass parts.

- Root position chords are generally used by default. Specific rules govern the use of inversions.

- Consecutive chords may not contain octaves or fifths (or equivalent compound intervals) between the same parts. For example, if one chord contains a fifth between the tenor and bass parts, the next chord may not also do so. This fault is known as parallel or consecutive fifths/octaves. To avoid this, the melody and bass line will usually be preserved while the inner parts are changed.

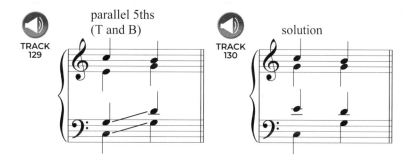

- The outer parts may not arrive at an octave or fifth in similar motion[13] where the soprano part moves by leap.[14] This fault is known as a hidden or exposed fifths/octaves.

- Attention should be paid to the horizontal aspect of the inner parts; if possible, they should also move in such a way as to be musically satisfactory in their own right, rather than jumping around seemingly at random to complete the harmony. In particular, certain notes should always move the way they seem to "want" to move. In general, inner notes should move to the nearest available note in the next chord. The leading note, in particular, should usually be followed by the tonic note if this is present in the chord. The subdominant note (IV) usually falls to the mediant (III). This general concept is known as voice leading.

- In order to preserve the identity of each part, overlaps between parts in consecutive chords are not allowed. In the next example, the bass note in the second chord overlaps with the tenor part in the first chord.

---

13 *Similar motion*: when two parts move in the same direction at the same time (both upwards to both downwards), as opposed to *contrary motion* (both parts moving in the opposite direction).

14 Movement by more than a second (whole tone or half tone) is considered a leap as opposed to a step.

TRACK 131

There are many other rules which are specific to particular harmonic contexts. In general, contrary motion between the outer parts is often considered more elegant than parallel motion, particularly when moving between chords built on adjacent steps (Eg. V–vi), as this helps avoid parallel fifths/octaves.

Cadences

The concept of *cadence* applies to almost all music with harmony, though it is most often discussed in the classical context. A cadence is a particular chord movement which acts as a musical punctuation mark. Just as there are different varieties of punctuation mark, cadences are usually divided into four types which are defined by the chords involved.

Perfect Cadence: V–I

This is the musical equivalent of a *full stop*, and is also known as a *full close*. The perfect cadence provides the most definite sense of completion at the end of a musical phrase. Note that the leading note (the third of chord V) must always resolve upwards to the tonic (the root note in chord I).

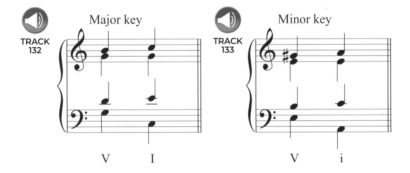

Plagal Cadence: IV–I

This has a similar function to a perfect cadence but with a slightly different musical character. Because of its association with church music, it is sometimes called an *amen cadence*.

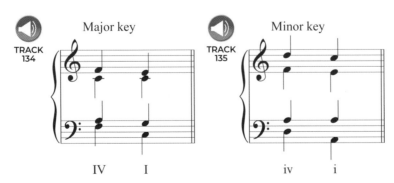

Imperfect Cadence: I–V

This is like a perfect cadence in reverse, and is like a musical comma; the musical statement does not seem to be finished because we have not yet reached the tonic chord. Other progressions such as ii–V, IV–V, and vi–V are also sometimes considered imperfect cadences.

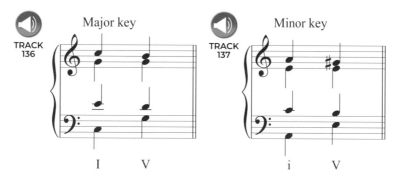

Interrupted Cadence: V–vi

Also known as a *deceptive cadence*, this cadence subverts our expectations; after chord V, we may be expecting chord I but instead land on chord vi, and so we have not yet come to rest. Because chord vi has two notes in common with chord I, the interrupted cadence may be used as an alternative harmonization to a melody that might otherwise imply a perfect cadence. Note that the third of chord VI is doubled, even in the minor key where it is a major chord, and is approached by contrary motion in different parts. This avoids consecutive fifths or octaves.

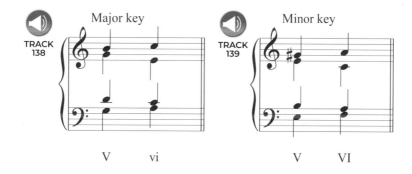

Basic Harmonization

The most straightforward way to harmonize a simple melody in the classical tradition is to treat all notes as harmony notes; each melody note is considered to belong to a chord. All diatonic root position chords which include the given note are available in principle, though chord vii is less commonly used, and choices may be limited by rules such as those outlined above. For example, if the melody moves from the root to the second, the chord sequence I–ii would certainly be avoided as it would include parallel octaves by definition.

Consider the following simple melody, assuming for now that it should start on chord I and end with a perfect cadence:

TRACK 140

This might be harmonized as follows:

TRACK 141

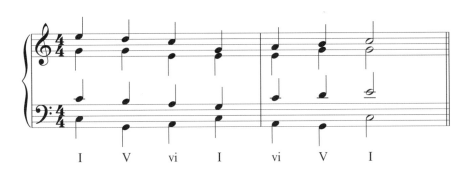

| I | V | vi | I | vi | V | I |

Note that parallel fifths and octaves are avoided here, and that contrary motion is achieved between chords V–vi (first measure) and vi–V (second measure).

Inversions

As in pop harmony, inversions are often used to enable stepwise bass motion, and as an additional means of avoiding parallel fifths or octaves.

TRACK 142

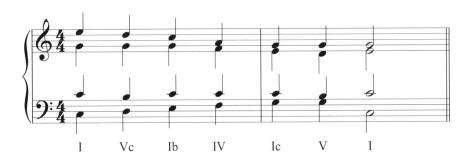

| I | Vc | Ib | IV | Ic | V | I |

CHAPTER 12
Chromatic Harmony and Modulation

Anything that happens within a tonal piece of music can be classified as either diatonic or chromatic. Diatonic simply means "of the key" or belonging to the key. *Chromatic*, from the Latin *chroma* (color), describes any note which is not strictly in the key, or any chord including at least one note from outside the key.

Modulation means to change key within a piece. There are many kinds of modulation: from abrupt to carefully prepared, temporary or permanent, to a near key or a far key.

Many kinds of modulation involve chromatic chords. Many chromatic chords work by implying a modulation. It therefore makes sense to consider chromatic harmony and modulation together.

The Dominant Seventh Chord

Dominant seventh chords strongly "want" to resolve to their tonic chord. In classical harmony, the leading note (which is the third of the dominant seventh) must always resolve upwards to the tonic. The subdominant (the seventh of the dominant seventh chord) resolves by a half step to the mediant (the third of the tonic chord). Because these two notes occur together in chord V7, following it with anything other than chord I tends to disrupt our expectations.

 TRACK 143

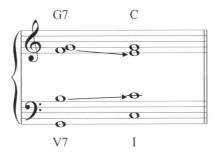

Secondary and Applied Dominants

A dominant seventh constructed on the supertonic (II7) is called a *secondary dominant*. It is chromatic because its third is major, which is not in the key. It resolves to the dominant chord in the key. For example, the secondary dominant in C major is D7. It contains the chromatic note F♯ which resolves to G (the dominant).

 TRACK 144

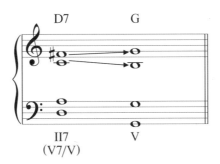

The dominant seventh chord type is often used as a chromatic chord precisely because it so strongly wants to resolve. Any chromatic dominant seventh chord which can resolve to a diatonic chord other than chord I is called an *applied dominant*. The following examples all show chromatic applied dominants which resolve to chords other than chord I in C major.

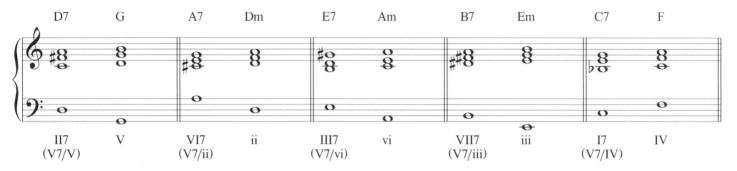

Many diatonic chord sequences with chords moving in fifths can be modified by the addition of one or more applied dominant sevenths. For example, the I–vi–ii–V progression:

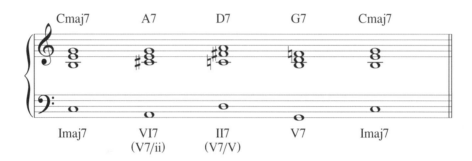

Modulation

Music may change key either temporarily or permanently by a variety of means, including the infamous "truck driver" key change often used for the final chorus of a pop song; the new key simply arrives, usually in the form of a new tonic chord a whole or half step above the original.

The type of modulation usually regarded as more satisfactory from classical harmony onwards involves the use of a *pivot chord* in the form of an applied dominant seventh (relative to the original key) which becomes the dominant seventh in the new key.

The following examples show the use of pivot chords when modulating to the relative minor, dominant, and subdominant keys. In each case, the pivot chord is shown both as a chromatic chord in the original key and as V7 in the new key.

Relative Minor (Example: C major to A minor)

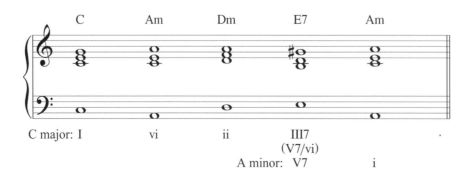

Dominant (Example: C major to G major)

TRACK 148

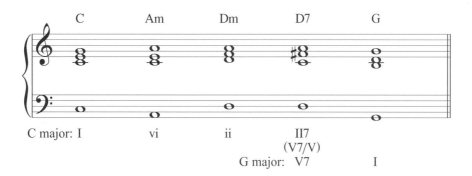

Subdominant (Example: C major to F major)

TRACK 149

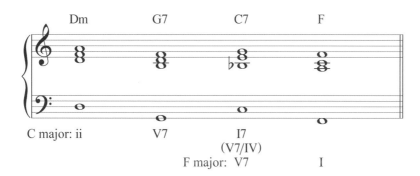

Other Chromatic Chords

A large number of chromatic chords are used across classical, jazz, and popular music, some of which are most easily analyzed as modified diatonic chords. Here are some of the most common:

iv

In the major key, chord IV may be modified by lowering its third to make it minor. This is often encountered directly after the major IV chord, but also often on its own, and is particularly effective as a poignant sounding ending (resolving to chord I). In jazz and early 20th century popular songs, it often appears as a minor sixth chord. The examples below show chord iv in two different contexts:

Listening:

Listen for the distinctive sound of chord iv in these songs:

- "In My Life" (The Beatles): "Some have gone..." moves from IV major to minor
- "Don't Look Back in Anger" (Oasis): "So I start a revolution..."
- "Bridge Over Troubled Water" (Simon & Garfunkel): penultimate chord
- "All By Myself" (Eric Carmen/Celine Dion): second chord of the verse—"...needed..."
- "Creep" (Radiohead): "Your skin makes me cry"

♭VII (Supertonic)

In a major key, the major chords formed on the flatted seventh step create a highly effective chromatic chord. The example below shows ♭VII combined with I, IV, and V in a typical rock sequence:

 TRACK 152

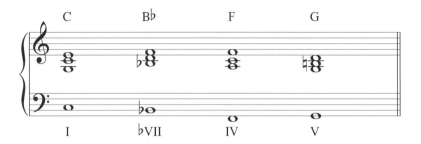

Listening:

- "Can't Get Enough" (Bad Company): I–♭VII–IV
- "I'm a Loser" (The Beatles) [verse]: I–V–♭VII–I
- "Firework" (Katy Perry): I–♭VII–vi–IV

♭VI (Flat Submediant)

The chord formed on the flatted sixth step in the major key is also frequently encountered. It can be viewed as being borrowed from the parallel minor key, and often forms an ascending progression with ♭VII leading to the tonic chord.

 TRACK 153

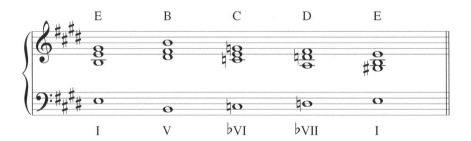

Listening:

- "Crazy Little Thing Called Love" (Queen): ♭VI–♭VII–I
- "Hey Joe" (Jimi Hendrix): ♭VI–♭III–♭VII–IV–I (also interesting as a cyclical progression)
- "Peggy Sue" (Buddy Holly): "Pretty, pretty, pretty…"
- "Airbag" (Radiohead): Intro

Augmented Sixth and ♭VI7 Chords

In classical harmony, there are three different *augmented sixth* chords, formed on the flatted submediant (sixth step) of either the major or minor key. The name refers to the interval between the outer notes. The three augmented sixth chords are shown here in C major (or C minor). Here, the augmented sixth interval is A♭–F♯.

 TRACK 154

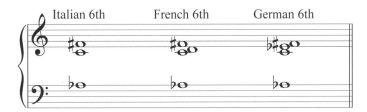

In jazz and pop harmony, the augmented sixth interval can be seen enharmonically as a minor seventh. The resulting chords can therefore be seen as chromatic dominant seventh chords (♭VI7), in fact, as tritone substitutes for the secondary dominant II7 chord (see Chapter 13). It is also interesting that, despite its origin in European classical harmony, the augmented sixth embodies a blues quality in a jazz/pop context and is a standard means of harmonizing the most dissonant *blue note* (the flatted fifth). The example below shows a II7–V7–I progression reharmonized in this way.[15]

 TRACK 155

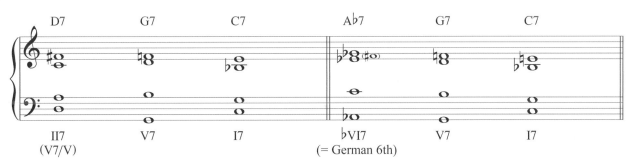

Listening:

- "Beautiful" (Carole King): penultimate chord of chorus
- "I Put a Spell on You" (Nina Simone): third chord of verse
- "Angel Eyes" (Matt Dennis): second chord

---

15 Classical harmony has stricter rules about the way an augmented sixth chord should resolve, so this connection is possibly tenuous, but the sound of the chord itself is the same.

Chromatic Chords at Work

When composing or arranging, "standard" chord sequences (see Chapter 10) can be made to sound more interesting by substituting one or more of the chords for a chromatic chord. Generally, the new chord will have at least one note in common with the original chord. Care should be taken not to introduce notes that clash with the melody, if this is already fixed.

For comparison, all of the sequences below are in C major.

I–vi–IV–V ("Stand by Me" sequence)

We have already seen that chord ii can be used in place of chord IV. Other possibilities include:
- iv (IV minor): C–Am(7)–Fm–G(7)
- II7 (chromatic secondary dominant): C–Am(7)–D7–G7

bVI7 (can be viewed as German sixth chord, or tritone substitute of II7. See Chapter 13): C–Am–Ab7–G7

I–V–vi–IV

This sequence can sound rather plain, but interesting possibilities are available as substitutions for the following chords:
- V: v (V minor) (Gm)
- V: bVII (Bb)
- vi: VI7 (A7)
- vi: bVI (Ab)
- vi: bVImaj7 (Abmaj7)
- vi: bVI7 (Ab7)
- IV: iv (IV minor) (Fm)

These ideas alone could result in a great many different sequences, for example:
- C–Gm–Am–Fm
- C–Bb–Ab–F
- C–G–A7–F

CHAPTER 13
Basics of Jazz Harmony

The following sections introduce a few concepts that are important to any understanding of jazz harmony.

Seventh Chords: Essential Notes

Though triads are the foundation of Western harmony, they are actually fairly rare in jazz. The characteristic flavor of jazz is provided by more complex chords from sevenths (four notes) and up; though as we shall see, not all notes of these chords are necessarily used at all times.

Jazz harmony leans very heavily on four types of seventh chord in particular: the major seventh (maj7), dominant seventh (7), minor seventh (m7), and half-diminished (m7♭5).

🔊 **TRACK 156**

With the exception of the half-diminished chord, all of these seventh chords contain a perfect fifth. However, this is often omitted by jazz performers and arrangers. Many pianists and guitarists also omit the root note in most situations. The essential notes of a seventh chord are therefore considered to be the third and the seventh (also known as *guide tones*).

🔊 **TRACK 157**

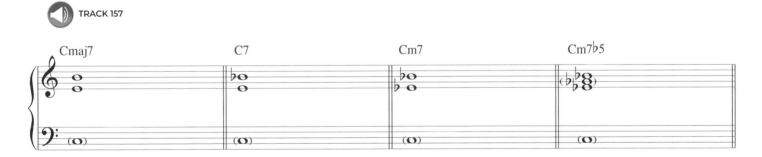

The ii–V Progression

The central progression in jazz is the ii–V. The example below shows this as a diatonic major progression resolving on the tonic chord (ii–V–I).

 TRACK 158

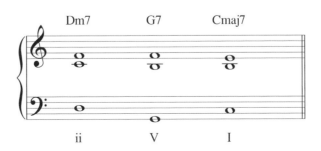

In the minor key, the ii chord is, strictly speaking, a half-diminished chord (m7♭5). Here it is more likely (though still not essential) that the fifth will be included to fully convey the minor key flavor.

 TRACK 159

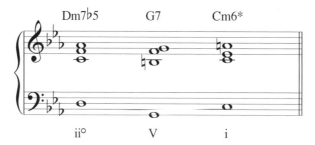

*The m6 chord is commonly used as a tonic minor chord.

This progression is often used chromatically. In this context, the dominant seventh chord is essentially an applied dominant, but the move is nonetheless often labelled as a ii–V, implying a temporary modulation. The sequence below is typical; the sequence, as a whole, is in G major. The first two chords may be viewed as a temporary modulation to A (major or minor), though the E7 is really an applied dominant chromatic chord in G major. The full progression can be analyzed in G major: iii–VI–ii–V–I.[16]

 TRACK 160

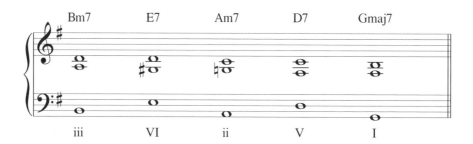

The ii–V progression is so strong that it forms the basis of many jazz standards. Duke Ellington's "Satin Doll" is a classic example:

SATIN DOLL
By DUKE ELLINGTON

Note that the A♭m7–D♭7 (measure 6), while a ii–V in itself, is an instance of tritone substitution in relation to the key center (see next page).

---

16   The first two chords in this progression are often analyzed as a ii–V in the key of D: (ii–V)–ii–V–I.

Voice Leading

For both improvising rhythm section players and arrangers, good voice leading is central to the implementation of jazz harmony. This means minimal movement between chord voicings. The third of the ii7 chord becomes the seventh of the V7 chord, and the seventh resolves downwards by a half step to the third of the dominant. For a sequence of ii–V chords, these voicings are transposed, and the motion is continued when resolving to a tonic chord.

 TRACK 162

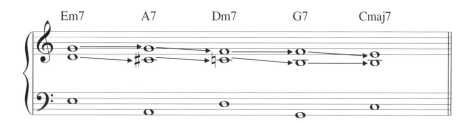

Further Applied Dominants

Dominant seventh-type chords are often used in place of the m7 ii chord in a ii–V progression. Where this is a modified diatonic ii–V progression, the resulting chord is the secondary dominant (chord V of V). With good voice leading, this chromatic chord sequence produces two chromatic descending lines. These are preserved through a cycle of II–V progression where all chords are dominant sevenths.

 TRACK 163

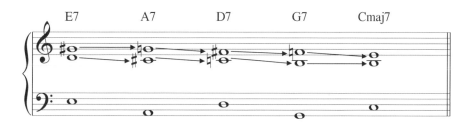

Tritone Substitution

The two essential notes of a dominant seventh chord happen to be a tritone (augmented fourth or diminished fifth) apart. Because these two inversions are enharmonic equivalents, any tritone interval is actually shared enharmonically between two different dominant seventh chords. For example, the essential notes in the chord of G7 are B (third) and F (seventh). If we respell either of these notes, we can instead see them as the seventh and third of alternative chords: D♭7 (C♭ and F) or C♯7 (B and E♯).

 TRACK 164

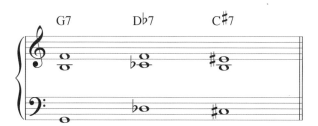

This phenomenon leads to the widespread practice in jazz of *tritone substitution*: switching one dominant seventh chord for the other chord which shares the same tritone (and also happens to be a tritone away). In its standard context, this changes a dominant chord whose root resolves down a fifth (or up a fourth) to one with its root note one half step above the chord of resolution.

 TRACK 165

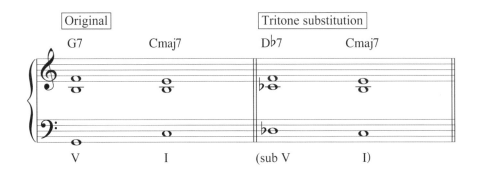

When applied to the ii–V–I progression, tritone substitution adds many possibilities. Whether the ii chord is a m7 or a chromatic 7 chord, it may either be left alone or transposed by a tritone.

Tritone Substitutions: ii–V–I Progressions (m7 ii Chord)

 TRACK 166

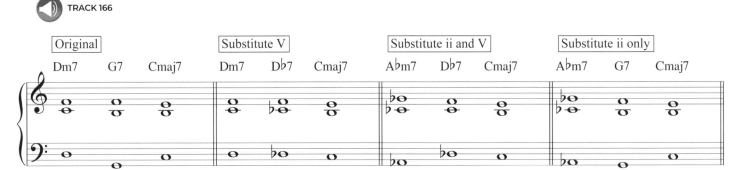

Tritone Substitutions: ii–V–I Progressions

 TRACK 167

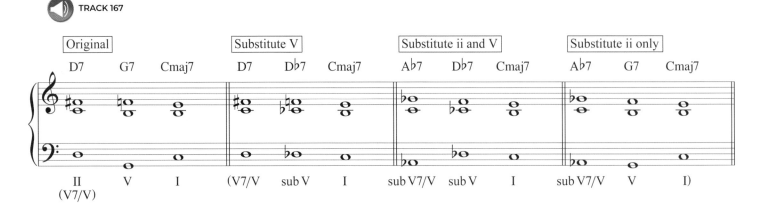

Substitutions in Practice

Many jazz performers and arrangers use tritone substitution throughout their work. Let's consider this in practice using the the first two bars of a standard jazz progression as an example: "Rhythm Changes," the harmonic framework for many jazz standards, named after George Gershwin's "I Got Rhythm."

In its original form, the first two bars of this sequence are a simple I–vi–ii–V progression (see Chapter 10). In the jazz idiom, these are usually rendered as (at least) seventh chords (m7 or 7).

TRACK 168

In many standards based on this progression, applied dominants are used in place of the diatonic m7 chords.

TRACK 169

Tritone substitution may be applied to any or all of the dominant seventh chords in the sequence. All of the possible combinations may be explored by finding the individual chord substitutions:

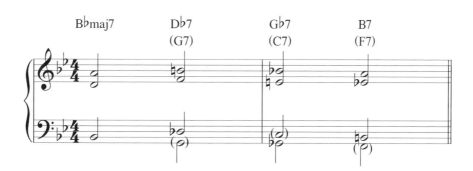

Note that as we are using essential chord notes only in the upper stave here, the notes do not change. Only the bass notes change, though enharmonic spellings could be used.

Natural and Altered Tension

We have seen that the third and seventh of a dominant seventh-type chord can be considered the essential notes. All other notes (apart from the root) that may be added to seventh chords may be considered as *tension* notes. This includes all types of ninths, 11ths, and 13ths.

Tension notes are usually grouped into two types: natural and altered. "Natural" implies that the note belongs to the major scale of which the seventh chord is the dominant; "altered" applies to all other notes. Taking the G7 family of chords as an example: Natural tension notes come from the C major scale, while altered tension notes do not.

While the natural fifth is not strictly a tension note, it tends to be classified as such both because it is a non-essential note and because all altered fifths definitely *are* tension notes.[17]

Ninth

The dominant ninth chord (symbol: 9) adds a natural tension ninth to the dominant seventh chord. Because the natural fifth also comes from the parent major scale, it may also be included without contradicting the flavor of the chord. This is largely a matter of style and context.

 TRACK 171

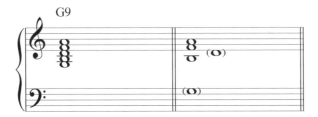

7♭9 and 7♯9

The dominant ninth chord may be altered by either lowering or raising the ninth by a half step. The resulting chord names are 7♭9 and 7♯9. The natural fifth may be included, depending on context, but is usually omitted as it tends to confuse the flavor of the chord.

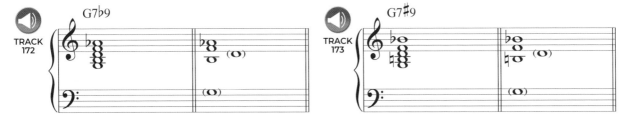

Thirteenth

Thirteenth chords (symbol: 13) add the natural 13th (sixth) to the dominant seventh chord. The essential notes are therefore the third, seventh, and 13th, but the natural fifth and ninth may also be included without contradicting the chord quality.

 TRACK 174

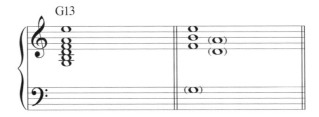

---

17   The flatted fifth/sharp 11th is sometimes considered to belong in both categories.

7♭13 or 7♯5

As the name implies, this is a dominant seventh with flatted 13th. Enharmonically, this is the same as a sharpened fifth.

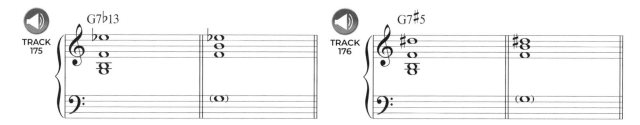

7♯11 or 7♭5

The natural 11th is not considered a tension note in the same sense as others, as the 11th (fourth) is more effectively used as a suspension (see Chapter 9). "7sus4" chords are therefore actually suspended chords that contain a seventh (and usually a ninth), but no third.

The sharpened 11th, however, is considered a tension note. Enharmonically, this is usually equivalent to a flatted fifth, though strictly speaking, a 7♯11 chord could also contain a natural fifth.

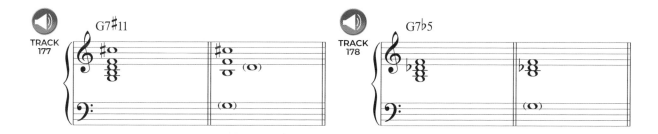

"Alt" Chord Symbol

Dense chords with many altered tension notes tend to result in very complex chord symbols if described fully. The *alt* symbol is sometimes used instead as a way to convey that the altered tension notes are appropriate, but the player may choose these according to taste (jazz is built on improvisation and many details are left to the player rather than dictated).

The following complex altered tension chords could also be more conveniently be labelled, using the alt symbol, such as "Galt" or "G7alt."

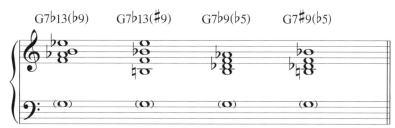

Mixed Tension

Whether natural or altered, tension notes are usually seen as belonging in either the ninths group (♭9, 9, ♯9) or the fifth/13ths group (from ♯11 to 13). Generally, natural tensions belong together, and altered tensions belong together. Departing from this creates even more dissonant and modern sounding chords containing both natural and altered tension simultaneously. These are known as *mixed tension chords*.

 TRACK 180

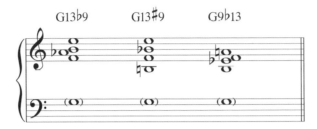

Functional Dominants, Tritone Substitution, and Swapping Tension

By convention, jazz performers, arrangers, and orchestrators mainly use altered tension where a dominant seventh-type chord is a functional dominant: one that resolves to a chord a perfect fifth below or perfect fourth above (for example G7–Cmaj7). This movement is so strong that the ear can reconcile the altered tension notes as chromatic without contradicting the basic V–I function.

Where a dominant seventh-type chord does not resolve in this way, natural tension notes tend to be used as the function of the chord is already chromatic.

When using the tritone substitute for a functional dominant chord, natural tension notes tend to be used where the original would have used altered tension notes. Another way to view this is that these are in fact the same notes; for example, consider the chords G7♭13 and D♭9, resolving to Cmaj7. Both contain the note E♭. This is altered tension (♭13) in relation to G7, but the natural tension ninth of D♭9. In both cases, it is a chromatic note in relation to the resolution chord. These tension notes often resolve most logically to upper extensions in the tonic chord. In the examples below, the E♭ resolves most satisfactorily to D, resulting in a Cmaj9 chord. Extending this line back to an E natural on ii chord results in Dm9.

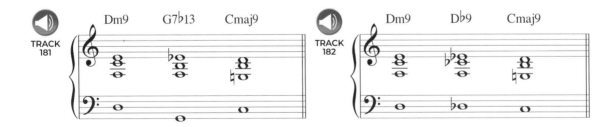

CHECKPOINT 6
Chord Sequences and Advanced Harmony

1. The following songs are listed in random order. Find the matches between the song titles and chord sequences below, and identify the sequence. One of them is a common variation on one of the sequences in Chapter 10 (the same chords in a different order). Other aspects such as the time signature, key, and rate of chord change will provide extra clues.

Songs:

- "ME!" (Taylor Swift)
  Words and Music by TAYLOR SWIFT, JOEL LITTLE and BRENDON URIE
  Copyright © 2019 Sony Music Publishing (US) LLC, Taylor Swift Music, EMI Blackwood Music Inc. and Listen To This Shhh
  All Rights on behalf of Sony Music Publishing (US) LLC, Taylor Swift Music and EMI Blackwood Music Inc. Administered by Sony Music Publishing (US) LLC, 424 Church Street, Suite 1200, Nashville, TN 37219
  All Rights on behalf of Listen To This Shhh Administered Worldwide by Kobalt Songs Music Publishing
  International Copyright Secured   All Rights Reserved

- "Without You" [chorus] (Harry Nilsson)
  Words and Music by PETER HAM and THOMAS EVANS
  Copyright © 1971 The Estate For Peter William Ham and The Estate For Thomas Evans
  Copyright Renewed
  All Rights Administered Worldwide by Kobalt Songs Music Publishing
  All Rights Reserved   Used by Permission

- "One of Us" [verse] (Joan Osborne)
  Words and Music by ERIC BAZILIAN
  © 1995 HUMAN BOY MUSIC
  All Rights Administered by WC MUSIC CORP.
  All Rights Reserved   Used by Permission

- "Still Got the Blues" (Gary Moore)
  Words and Music by GARY MOORE
  Copyright © 1990 Bonuswise Ltd.
  All Rights Administered by BMG Rights Management (US) LLC
  All Rights Reserved   Used by Permission

- "Pencil Full of Lead" (Paolo Nutini)
  Words and Music by PAOLO NUTINI
  © 2009 WARNER/CHAPPELL MUSIC LTD.
  All Rights in the U.S. and Canada Administered by WC MUSIC CORP.
  All Rights Reserved   Used by Permission

Chord Sequences:

- A:

- B:

- C:

- D:

• E:

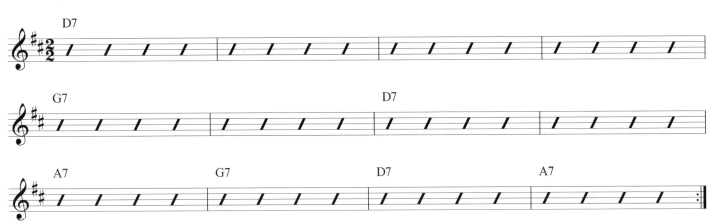

2. For each example below, identify the key, analyze the chord using Roman numerals, and name the cadence (perfect, imperfect, plagal, or interrupted).

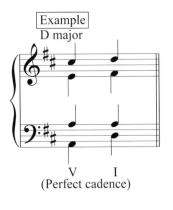

Example
D major

V   I
(Perfect cadence)

3. Each classical harmony example below contains one error in the form of parallel fifths or octaves. Find the error in each case, identifying the parts between which it occurs.

4. Each of these chord sequences below modulates as stated, but the pivot chord (dominant seventh of the new key) is omitted. Add the name of the chord and place its notes on the stave using good voice leading to connect with the chords on either side.

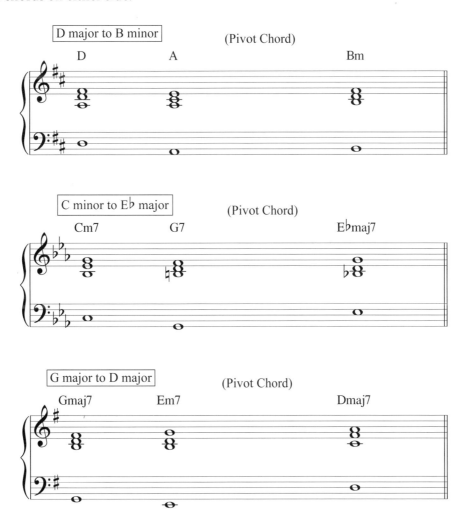

5. Using chord names only, identify the diatonic ii–V seventh chords that resolve to the following I chords:

- Abmaj7

- Cm6

- Dmaj7

- Fm6

- Bbm7

- Gmaj7

- Dbmaj7

6. Add the missing chord names to the chord sequences below:

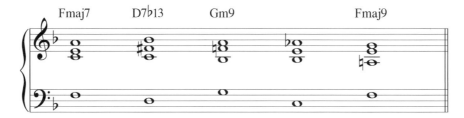

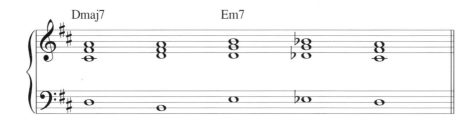

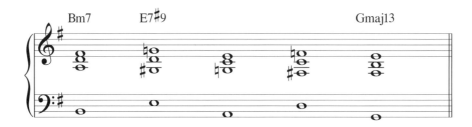

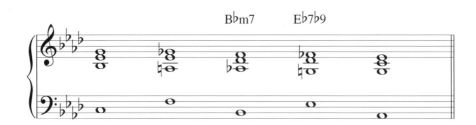

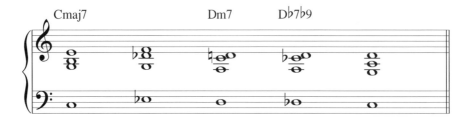

CONCLUSION

If you have absorbed the information and ideas within this book, you will have built a solid foundation on which to base your further musical studies. In all areas, this is of course not the end of the line—generally, the more you learn, the more there is to learn. Fortunately, available resources to this end are more accessible than ever, ranging from further reading to a huge amount of online material. Coupled with the easy ability to listen to almost anything ever released, this makes it easier than ever to keep making unforeseen connections between styles and eras in the pursuit of interesting new music and to forge a unique and powerful identity for yourself as a musician.

CHECKPOINT ANSWERS

Checkpoint 1

1. Sixteenth (1/4 beat), quarter (one beat), 64th (1/16 beat), half (two beats), eighth (1/2 beat), 32nd (1/8 beat), whole (four beats)

2.

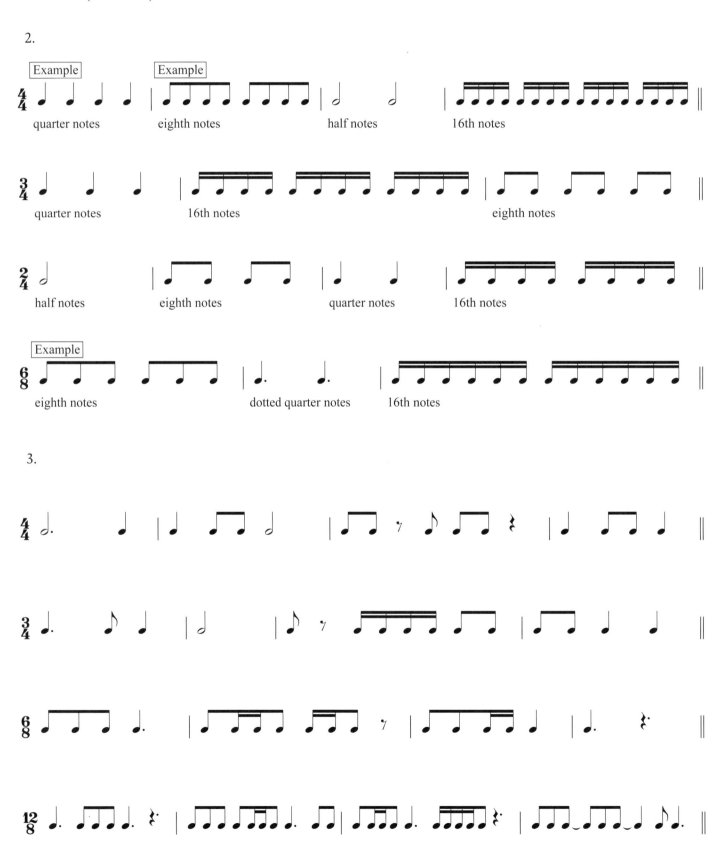

3.

4.

5.

6. Seal: "Kiss From a Rose" _____ $\frac{3}{4}$

Robert Palmer: "Addicted to Love" _____ $\frac{4}{4}$

Paul Simon: "Have a Good Time" _____ $\frac{7}{4}$

Holst: "Mars, The Bringer of War" (from *The Planets*) __ $\frac{5}{4}$

Pat Metheny & Charlie Haden: "Spiritual" _____ $\frac{6}{8}$

7. MC5: "Sister Anne"—142

Chic: "Le Freak"—120

Charlie Parker: "Donna Lee"—230

The Blue Nile: "Over the Hillside"—55

Neil Young: "Only Love Can Break Your Heart"—110

Taylor Swift/Bon Iver: "Exile"—72

Green Day: "Basket Case"—175

James Taylor: "Music"—82

Philip Glass: "Glassworks I - Opening"—92

Checkpoint 2

1.

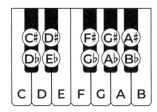

2.

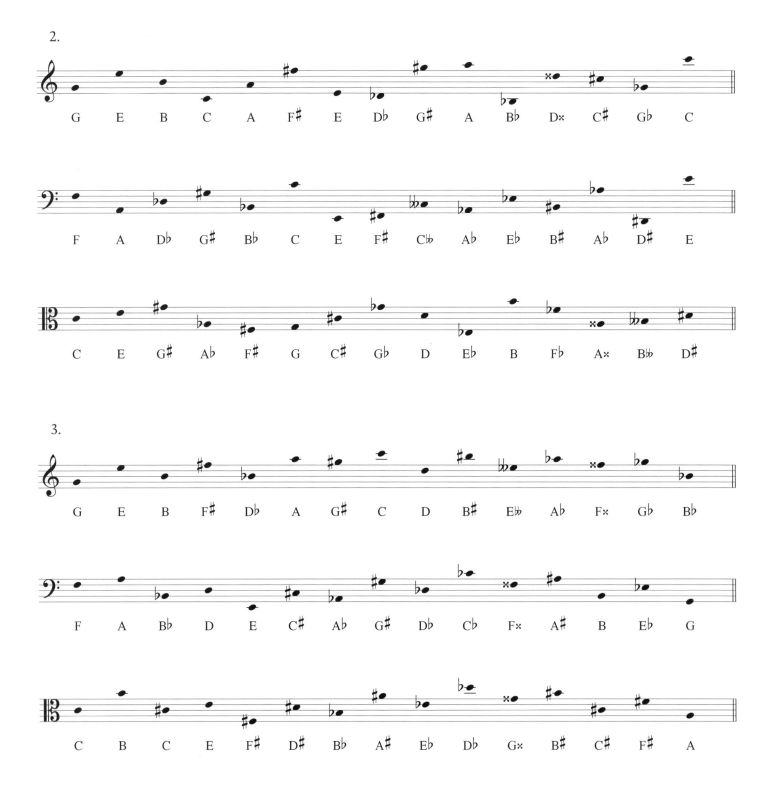

4.

Checkpoint 3

1.

- A major: F# minor
- F major: D minor
- D major: B minor
- B♭ major: G minor

- F# major: D# minor
- A♭ major: F minor
- C minor: E♭ major
- G# minor: B major

- E minor: G major
- C# minor: E major
- B♭ minor: D♭ major
- E♭ minor: G♭ major

2. A major/F# minor; A♭ major/F minor; G major/E minor; B♭ major/G minor
   E major/C# minor; F major/D minor; D major/B minor; C♭ major/A♭ minor
   B major/G# minor; C major/A minor; C# major/A# minor; E♭ major/C minor

3. B♭ major: B♭–C–D–E♭–F–G–A–B♭.
   F major: F–G–A–B♭–C–D–E–F.
   A major: A–B–C#–D–E–F#–G#–A.
   A♭ major: A♭–B♭–C–D♭–E♭–F–G–A♭.
   B major: B–C#–D#–E–F#–G#–A#–B.
   G♭ major: G♭–A♭–B♭–C♭–D♭–E♭–F–G♭.
   C natural minor: C–D–E♭–F–G–A♭–B♭–C.
   G# natural minor: G#–A#–B–C#–D#–E–F#–G#.
   A harmonic minor: A–B–C–D–E–F–G#–A.
   C harmonic minor: C–D–E♭–F–G–A♭–B–C.
   F# harmonic minor: F#–G#–A–B–C#–D–E#–F#.
   C# melodic minor: C#–D#–E–F#–G#–A#–B#–C#–B♮–A♮–G#–F#–E–D#–C#.
   G melodic minor: G–A–B♭–C–D–E–F#–G–F♮–E♭–D–C–B♭–A–G.
   F melodic minor: F–G–A♭–B♭–C–D–E–F–E♭–D♭–C–B♭–A♭–G–F.

4.

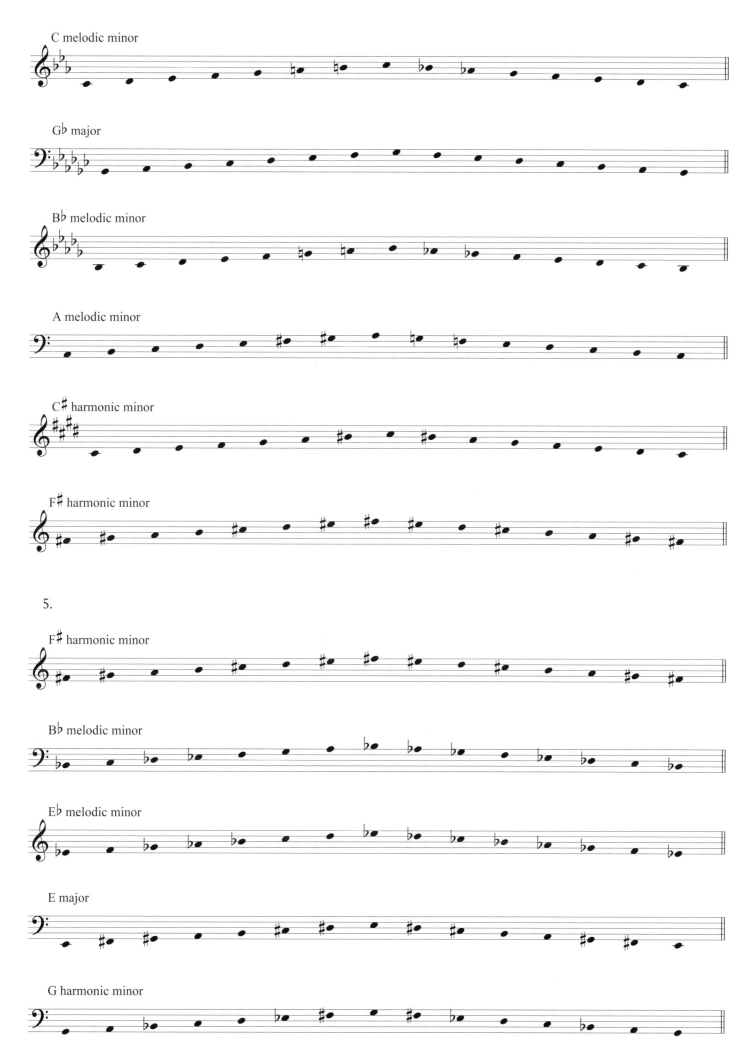

C melodic minor

G♭ major

B♭ melodic minor

A melodic minor

C♯ harmonic minor

F♯ harmonic minor

5.

F♯ harmonic minor

B♭ melodic minor

E♭ melodic minor

E major

G harmonic minor

G harmonic minor

B melodic minor

A major

D♭ major

F melodic minor

6.

Example

Key: C major
Note: G natural
Step: V/dominant

Key: G major
Note: F sharp
Step: vii/leading note

Key: D major
Note: B natural
Step: vi/submediant

Key: F sharp major
Note: G sharp
Step: ii/supertonic

Key: C sharp major
Note: E sharp
Step: iii/mediant

Key: E flat major
Note: A flat
Step: IV/subdominant

Key: A flat major
Note: C natural
Step: iii/mediant

Key: D flat major
Note: E flat
Step: ii/supertonic

Key: A major
Note: A natural
Step: I/tonic

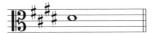

Key: E major
Note: D sharp
Step: vii/leading note

Key: B major
Note: E natural
Step: IV/subdominant

Key: G flat major
Note: C flat
Step: IV/subdominant

Key: C flat major
Note: G flat
Step: V/dominant

Key: F major
Note: D natural
Step: vi/submediant

Key: B flat major
Note: A natural
Step: vii/leading note

Checkpoint 4

1.

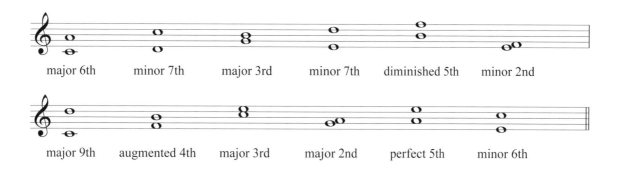

major 6th   minor 7th   major 3rd   minor 7th   diminished 5th   minor 2nd

major 9th   augmented 4th   major 3rd   major 2nd   perfect 5th   minor 6th

2.

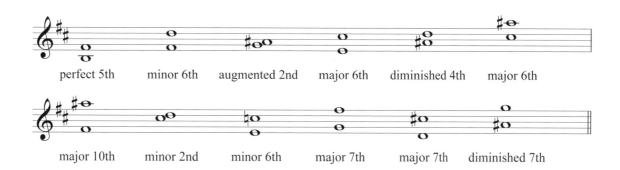

perfect 5th   minor 6th   augmented 2nd   major 6th   diminished 4th   major 6th

major 10th   minor 2nd   minor 6th   major 7th   major 7th   diminished 7th

3.

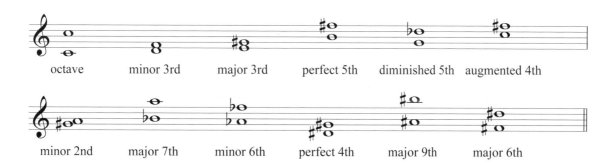

octave   minor 3rd   major 3rd   perfect 5th   diminished 5th   augmented 4th

minor 2nd   major 7th   minor 6th   perfect 4th   major 9th   major 6th

4.

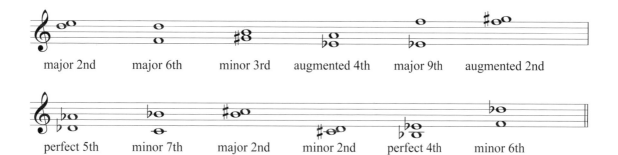

major 2nd   major 6th   minor 3rd   augmented 4th   major 9th   augmented 2nd

perfect 5th   minor 7th   major 2nd   minor 2nd   perfect 4th   minor 6th

5.

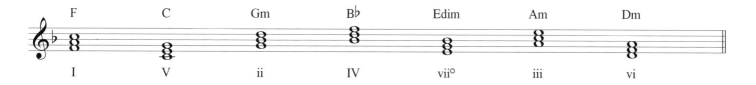

F   C   Gm   Bb   Edim   Am   Dm

I   V   ii   IV   vii°   iii   vi

6.

7.

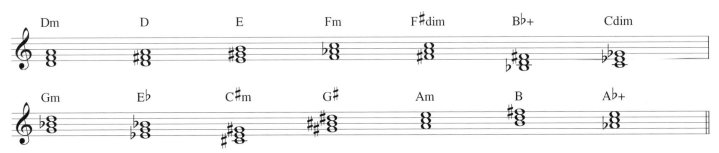

8.

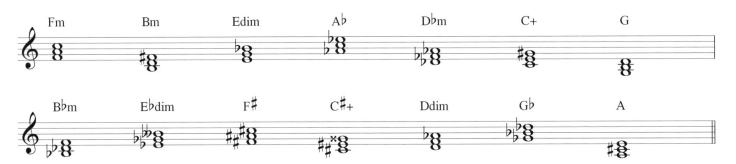

9.

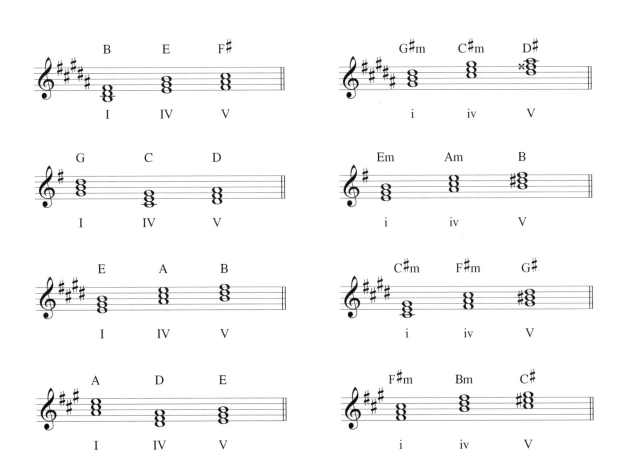

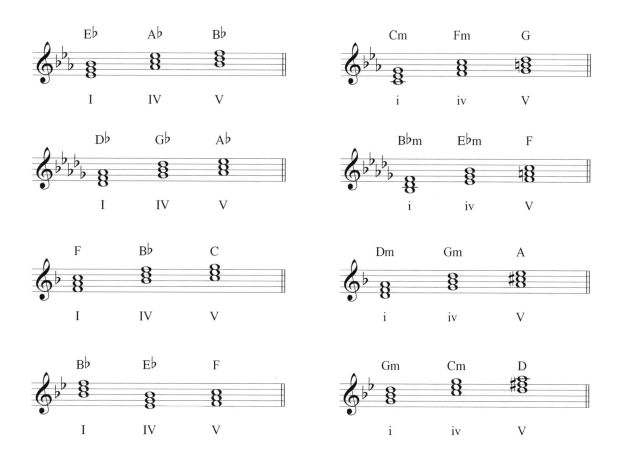

Checkpoint 5

4.

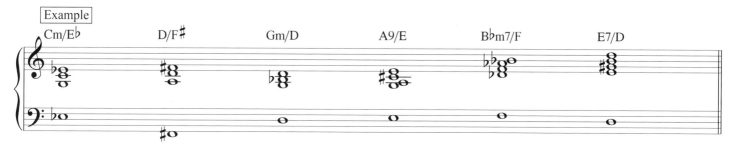

5.

C/E
(example)

G7/F   Fm/A♭   B7/F♯   E♭m/B♭   Gmaj7/C

Checkpoint 6

1. "ME!": sequence C (I–vi–IV–V in C major)

   "Without You": sequence D (I–vi–ii–V in E major)

   "One of Us": sequence B (vi–VI–I–V in A major. This is a re-ordered version of I–V–vi–IV.)

   "Still Got the Blues": sequence A (cyclical sequence in C/A minor)

   "Pencil Full of Lead": sequence E (12-bar blues in D major)

2.

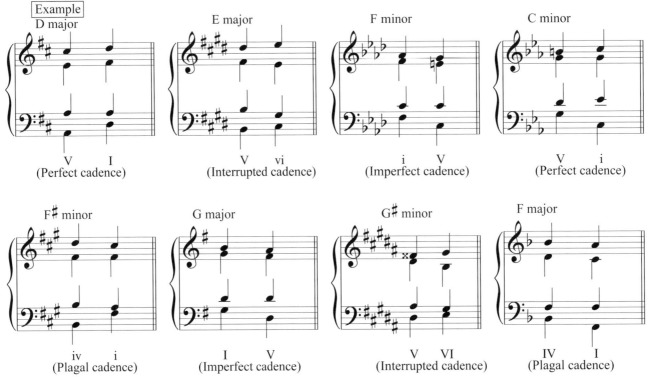

3.

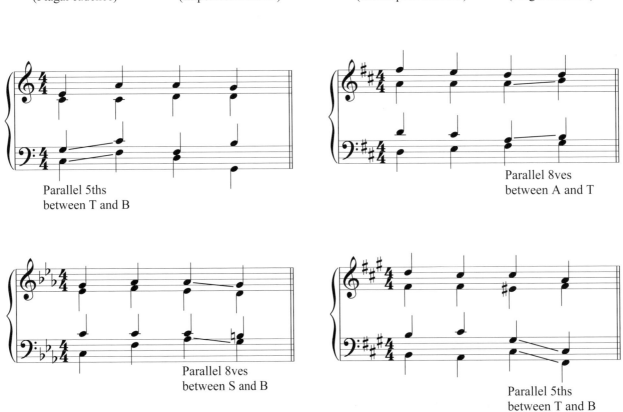

4.

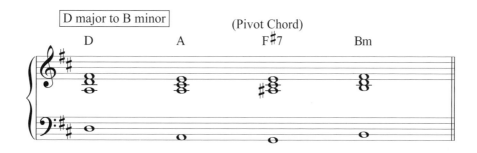

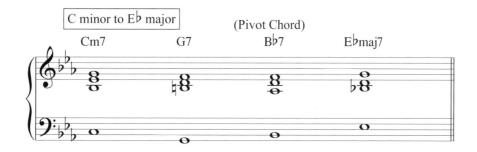

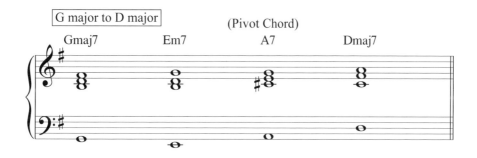

5.   Bbm7–Eb7–Abmaj7
     Dm7(b5)–G7–Cm6
     Em7–A7–Dmaj7
     Gm7(b5)–C7–Fm6
     Cm7(b5)–F7–Bbm7
     Am7–D7–Gmaj7
     Ebm7–Ab7–Dbmaj7

6.

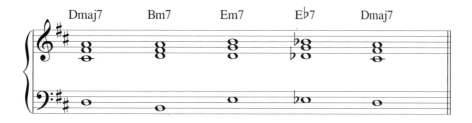

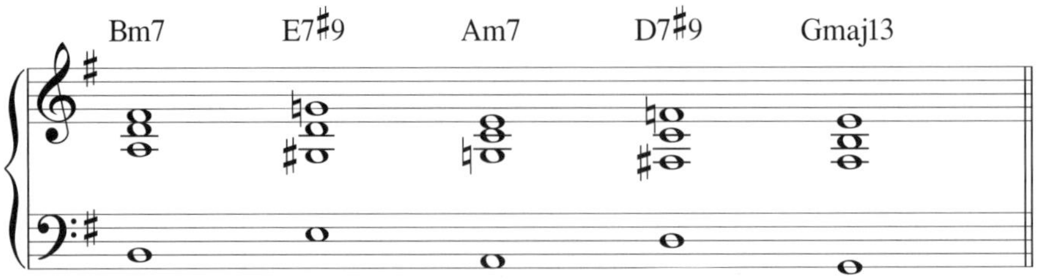
Bm7
E7♯9
Am7
D7♯9
Gmaj13

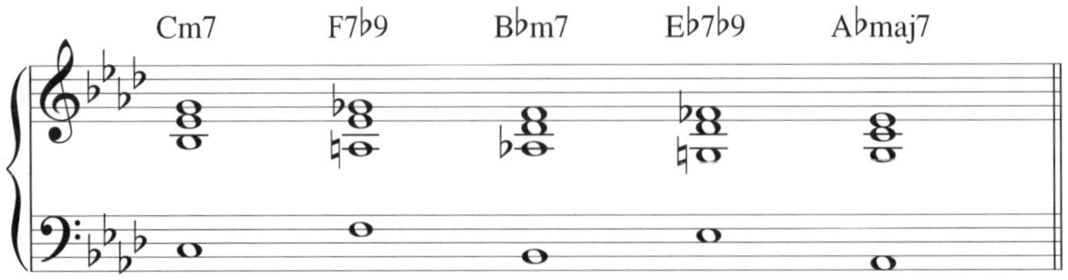
Cm7
F7♭9
B♭m7
E♭7♭9
A♭maj7

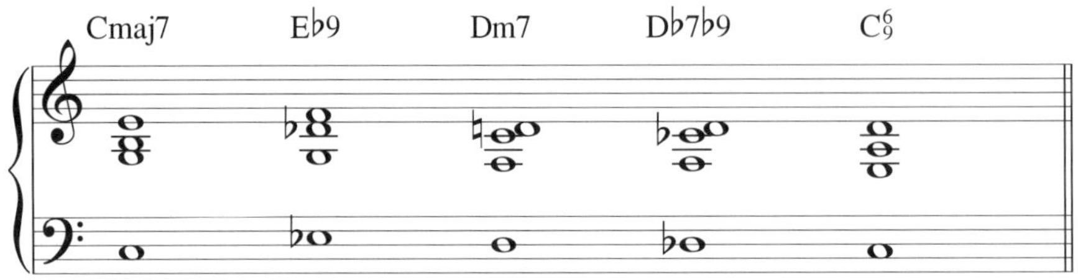
Cmaj7
E♭9
Dm7
D♭7♭9
C6/9

GLOSSARY OF TERMS

415 Hz	("Baroque pitch") The reference frequency often used to define the pitch of the note A above middle C in historically informed performance of Baroque (and earlier) musical styles. Approximately a half step lower than 440 Hz.
440 Hz	("Modern pitch") The reference frequency used to define the pitch of the note A above middle C for most modern music, instruments, and orchestras.
Accidental	A sharp, flat, or natural symbol placed to the left of a note which usually indicates that it is modified relative to that defined by the key signature. For example, to use a B♭ in C major (which has no sharps or flats) or an F natural in G major (which includes F♯).
Aeolian Mode	The sixth mode of the major scale, and an alternative name for the natural minor scale. In parallel terms, the Aeolian mode can be seen as a major scale with a flatted third, flatted sixth, and flatted seventh.
Alto	(Abbreviation of *contralto*) 1) The second-highest standardized human voice range, usually sung by female voices. 2) The second-highest part in four-part harmony, and thus one of the inner parts.
Alto Clef	A clef used for viola music and occasionally for other instruments. On a five-line stave, the alto clef defines the middle line as middle C.
Anacrusis	The use of a partial measure to begin a piece on anything other than beat 1.
Atonality	Music written without a tonal center or key, generally associated with classical composers of the early 20th century onwards. See *serialism*.
Augmented Chord/Triad	A three-note chord having a major third and augmented fifth from the root note. Spelling: 1–3–♯5. Symbol: aug, + (e.g. Caug, Aaug, C+, A+).
Augmented Interval	An interval which is one half step wider than either a perfect or major interval.
Bar	(International English) *measure*
Bar Line	A vertical line separating measures in musical notation.
Bass	The lowest standardized human voice range, usually sung by male voices. 2) The lowest part in four-part harmony. 3) Often used as an abbreviation/informal term for any instrument used to cover this range, for example bass guitar, double bass, or tuba. 4) See also *bass note*.
Bass Clef	The clef most often used for bass instruments. On a five-line stave, the bass defines the second line down as F below middle C.

Bass Note	The lowest sounding note of a chord or musical texture.
Beat	A single pulse event in music.
Bitonality	Describes music written in two keys at once. For example, two instruments in different keys or different keys for the each hand of a piano part. See also *polytonality*.
Blue Note	One of a number of notes which give blues and derived styles their musical character, defined in parallel terms with reference to the major scale. In early blues, the flatted third and flatted seventh created dissonance when combined with primary triads in the major key. These dissonances were gradually assimilated into blues tonality through the use of dominant seventh chords. Later, the more persistent dissonance of the flatted fifth became the third standardized blue note.
Blues Scale	A somewhat contested term, the blues scale is most commonly taken to consist of the minor pentatonic with the addition of the extra blue note, the flatted fifth: 1–♭3–4–♭5–5–♭7).
Breve	(International English) *double whole note*
Cadence	A moment of musical punctuation consisting of two chords. See *perfect cadence, plagal cadence, interrupted cadence, imperfect cadence.*
Cesura	A symbol usually constructed of two diagonal lines (//), indicating that the pulse should be paused until the conductor or musical director indicates to move on. Often encountered in musical theater writing. Also known informally as "tramlines."
Chord	The result of any two or more non-identical pitches (not counting octaves) sounding together, whether on a single instrument or within an ensemble.
Chord Quality	This describes the internal construction of a chord, as opposed to the root note it is built on. Examples include major, minor, diminished, etc.
Chord Spelling	A system for defining the notes of any chord type relative to the numbered steps of the major scale. Numbers without accidentals represent intervals found in the major scale while sharps and flats are used as modifiers. For example, 3 represents a major third while ♭3 denotes a minor third. The a major triad is spelled 1–3–5 while a minor seventh chord is 1–♭3–5–♭7. See also *parallel scale/mode*.
Chord Symbol	A system of notating harmony, used both to instruct players of chordal instruments (such as the guitar) and for musical analysis. The chord symbol may specify the root note, chord quality, and, optionally by means of a slash, the use of a note other than the root as a bass note (indicating either an inversion or a more complex chord). Examples: C (C major), Dm (D minor), E♭7 (E♭ dominant seventh).
Chromatic	A phrase or chord containing notes from outside the key (in contrast to *diatonic*).
Clef	The symbol usually placed first on the stave in any line of music, to specify the absolute location of pitches in use. See *treble clef, bass clef, alto clef, tenor clef*.
Coda	Italian for "tail." An ending written separately after the main body of a piece, usually reached by first repeating part of the piece. See *D.C.* and *D.S.* Symbol: ⊕
Complementary Intervals	Two intervals which comprise an octave in total.

Compound Interval	An interval greater than one octave which is harmonically equivalent to one or more octaves plus a smaller interval. For example, a major tenth may be considered equivalent to a major third.
Compound Time	A meter or time signature where the basic pulse is divided by three rather than two. Each beat is represented by a dotted quarter note which further divides into three eighth notes. Examples: 6/8, 9/8, 12/8. See also *simple time*.
Concert Pitch	A loose concept used to define a pitch reference so that musicians may sound in tune together. This has varied historically, but in modern use is usually A=440Hz (modern pitch) or 415Hz (Baroque pitch). Also used to refer to the names of notes on non-transposing instruments.
Consecutive Fifth	See *parallel fifth*.
Consecutive Octave	See *parallel octave*.
Consonance	Describes the effect of two or more notes sounding together resulting in a relatively pleasant or sweet effect, contrasting with *dissonance*.
Contralto	See *alto*.
Contrary Motion	The occurrence of two or more musical parts (particularly outer parts) moving in opposite directions (ascending or descending) at the same time.
Cross-Rhythm	The interruption of the expected pulse using a rhythm or phrase that falls on a different point within the meter each time it is repeated. For example, a pattern of three eighth notes in 4/4 will fall on beat 1, then the second half of beat 2, then beat 4, then the second half of beat 1, and so on, and will only fall on beat 1 again after three bars.
Crotchet	(International English) *quarter note*
D.C.	Abbreviation of *Da Capo*. An instruction to return to the beginning of a piece, usually taking one of two forms: *D.C. al Coda* (return to the beginning, then jump to the coda at a point specified by the indication *To Coda*) or *D.C. al Fine* (return to the beginning and play as far as the indication *Fine* (end).
D.S.	Abbreviation of *Dal Segno*. An instruction to return a point marked by the *segno*, usually taking one of two forms: *D.S. al Coda* (return to the sign, then jump to the coda at a point specified by the indication *To Coda*) or *D.S. al Fine* (return to the sign and play as far as the indication *Fine* (end).
Demisemiquaver	(International English) *32nd note*
Diatonic	Belonging to a key. See also *chromatic*.
Diminished Chord/Triad	A three-note chord having a minor third and diminished fifth from the root note. Spelling: 1–♭3–♭5. Symbol: ° (e.g. C°, A°).
Diminished Interval	An interval which is one half step narrower than either a perfect or minor interval.
Dissonance	The effect of two or more notes sounding together with a relatively unpleasant effect, though this depends greatly on context. Contrast with *consonance*.

Dominant Seventh Chord	A seventh chord containing a major third, perfect fifth, and minor seventh from the root (1–3–5–♭7). Found as chord V7 (the dominant) in major and (harmonic) minor tonality. Chord symbol: 7 (e.g. C7, A7)
Dorian Mode	The second mode of the major scale. In parallel terms, the Dorian mode can be seen as a major scale with a flatted third and flatted seventh.
Double Whole Note	A note value rarely encountered in modern use, having twice the value of a whole note. ‖O‖
Duple Time	A time signature in which two primary pulses are felt.
Dynamics	The consideration of musical volume or loudness. Dynamic markings may indicate that one section of music is louder or quieter than another, that some instruments are louder or quieter than others at any given time, or that either of these aspects is to change gradually or suddenly over time.
Eighth Note	A note having an eighth of the duration of a whole note. ♪
Eleventh Chord	A chord which may contain a third, fifth, seventh, ninth, and 11th from the root note. The dominant 11th (symbol: 11; spelling: 1–(3)–5–♭7–9–11) usually omits the third, as the 11th (fourth) can act as a suspension. The minor 11th (symbol: m11; spelling: 1–♭3–5–7–9–11–13) contains a minor third but often omits the ninth.
Enharmonic Equivalent	The description of a note, chord root, or interval in a different context using an alternative but physically identical term. Examples (note names or chord roots): F♯=G♭, C♭=B). Examples (intervals): minor sixth = augmented fifth, major sixth = diminished seventh.
Equal Temperament	The modern system of dividing the octave into twelve exactly equal half steps, so that each half step is defined by the frequency ratio $1:2^{1/12}$ (one to the twelfth root of two). See *temperament*.
Fermata	See *pause mark*.
Fifth (interval)	An interval encompassing five note names. For example, C–G. Commonly either perfect (seven half steps), diminished (six half steps), or augmented (eight half steps).
Figured Bass	A historical system to show harmony in relation to a bass line, where numbers are used to denote the intervals required to construct chords above a given bass note.
Fine	A marking showing the end of a piece, usually placed to indicate that the performance should end partway through the section, having previously played past this point and back to the beginning (*D.C.*) or sign (*D.S.*).
First Inversion	A chord where the third is used as the bass note. For example, a C major chord with E in the bass.
Flat	The ♭ symbol, placed to the left of a note as an accidental, or in the key signature, to indicate that a given note (which would otherwise be a natural) should be lowered by a half step.
f	*Dynamic* marking: *forte* (loud).

Four-Part Harmony	The discipline of writing music in four parts (soprano, alto, tenor, bass) corresponding to standardized human voice ranges, whether for vocal/choral music or as a basis for instrumental orchestration. As a cornerstone of common practice, subject to strict rules.
Fourth (interval)	An interval encompassing four note names. For example, C–F. Commonly either perfect (five half steps) or augmented (six half steps).
Frequency	A measure of the pitch of a note, or harmonic component of a note, in cycles per second or Hertz (Hz).
Fundamental	The lowest frequency present in any pitched sound more complex than a sine wave. Other frequencies are usually harmonics or partials mathematically related to the fundamental.
Generic Interval	An interval defined only by the number of scale steps or letter names encompassed, and therefore not fully defined. See also *specific interval*.
H	In German and some other Germanic languages, the note called B in English is called H, and B♭ is called B.
Half Note	A note having half the duration of a whole note. Represents one beat in all time signatures where the lower number is 2 (e.g. 2/2, 3/2).
Harmonic Minor Scale	A minor scale in which the seventh is raised by a half step compared with the natural minor scale, mainly used as the basis of minor key harmony in Western classical music.
Harmonic Series	A series of mathematically related frequencies present in varying proportions alongside the fundamental in most pitched instrument sounds, where these proportions play a large part in determining the timbre of the instrument.
Hemiola	The phenomenon created by three musical phrases in the time of two. For example, three two-beat phrases in triple time.
Hidden Fifth	An occurence in counterpoint in which two voices, distanced by a non-fifth interval, move in similar motion to produce a fifth in the next chord.
Homophony	Music where all parts move together in the same rhythm. Usually, a melody part is supported by one or more additional parts which define the harmony. (Adjective: *homophonic*). Contrasts with *polyphony*.
Imperfect Cadence	A cadence where the second chord is chord V. The simplest form is I–V, but various chords may be used as the first chord.
Inner Parts	The parts other than the lowest and highest in a musical texture. In four-part harmony, the alto and tenor parts.
Interrupted Cadence	A cadence consisting of the chord progression V–VI.
Interval	A measure of the difference in pitch between two notes.
Inversion	A chord where a note other than the root is used as the bass note; usually represented as a slash chord in chord symbol notation. See *first/second/third inversion*, *root position*.
Ionian Mode	Alternative name for the *major scale*.

Key	The family of pitches that forms the basis of a piece of music, as expressed in a *scale* or *mode*.
Key Signature	The arrangement of sharp or flat symbols (or neither) which defines the musical key in use by specifying which notes on the stave are to be played as sharps or flats without the use of accidentals. Key signatures are usually placed at the start of each line after the clef, but may also be placed anywhere where a change of key is required, usually before a bar line.
Largo	Italian term for "slow"; often used as a tempo marking.
Locrian Mode	The seventh mode of the major scale. In parallel terms, the Locrian mode can be seen as a major scale with flatted second, third, fifth, sixth, and seventh steps.
Lydian Mode	The fourth mode of the major scale. In parallel terms, the Lydian mode can be seen as a major scale with a raised fourth.
Major Chord/Triad	A three-note chord having a major third and perfect fifth from the root note. Spelling: 1–3–5. Symbol: root name only (e.g. C, A).
Major Interval	An interval which is one half step wider than the corresponding minor interval. Seconds, thirds, sixths, and sevenths (and their compound intervals) may be defined as major or minor.
Major Scale	The scale at the heart of the Western major/minor key system, and the basis for most other Western scales and modes. The major scale is constructed using a combination of whole and half steps: W–W–H–W–W–W–H.
Major Seventh Chord	A seventh chord containing a major third, perfect fifth, and major seventh from the root (1–3–5–7). Found as chord I7 and IV7 in major tonality and chord VI in minor keys. Chord symbol: maj7 (e.g. Cmaj7, Amaj7).
Major Sixth Chord	A sixth chord containing a major third, perfect fifth, and major sixth from the root (1–3–5–6). Chord symbol: 6 (e.g. C6, A6).
Measure	A basic unit of pulse in musical notation where each measure contains a number of beats as determined by the meter, separated by bar lines.
Melodic Minor Scale	In the classical tradition, this scale is derived by raising the sixth and seventh steps of the natural minor scale by a half step when ascending, but reverting back to the natural minor when descending. In jazz, only the ascending form is considered and practiced in both directions. The ascending/jazz form may be analyzed in parallel terms as a major scale with a minor third (1–2–♭3–4–5–6–7).
Meter	The organization of musical pulse into a (usually) repetitive number of beats, as defined by a time signature.
mf	*Dynamic* marking: *mezzoforte* (moderately loud).
mp	*Dynamic* marking: *mezzopiano* (moderately soft).
Middle C	A note often used as a fixed reference relative to other notes, middle C is the C closest to the center of a full-size piano keyboard. At modern pitch (A=440Hz) and equal temperament.
Minim	(International English) *half note*
Minor Chord/Triad	A three-note chord having a minor third and perfect fifth from the root note. Spelling: 1–♭3–5. Symbol: m (e.g. Cm, Am).

Minor Interval	An interval which is one half step narrower than the corresponding major interval. Seconds, thirds, sixths, and sevenths (and their compound intervals) may be defined as major or minor.
Minor Scale	A general term for one of several scales derived from the major scale: the natural minor, harmonic minor, and melodic minor.
Minor Seventh Chord	A seventh chord containing a minor third, perfect fifth, and minor seventh from the root (1–♭3–5–♭7). Chord symbol: m7 (e.g. Cm7, Am7).
Minor Sixth Chord	A sixth chord containing a minor third, perfect fifth, and major sixth from the root (1–♭3–5–6). Chord symbol: 6 (e.g. C6, A6).
Mixolydian Mode	The fifth mode of the major scale. In parallel terms, the Mixolydian mode can be seen as a major scale with a flatted seventh.
Mode	A type of scale and tonality derived from another scale, sharing the same set of notes but with a different key center.
Natural	The ♮ symbol, placed to the left of a note as an accidental, indicated that a given note (which would otherwise be a sharp or flat as defined by the key signature or sharp/flat symbol earlier in the measure) should be played as a natural (white note) instead.
Natural Minor Scale	The name usually used for the Aeolian Mode in the Western classical tradition. The natural minor scale shares the same set of notes as its relative major scale, without modification (see *harmonic minor scale* and *melodic minor scale*).
Ninth Chord	A chord constructed with a third, fifth, seventh, and ninth from the root (though the fifth may be omitted). Types of ninth chord include the dominant ninth (symbol: 9; spelling: 1–3–5–♭7–9), major ninth (symbol: maj9; spelling: 1–3–5–7–9) and minor ninth (symbol: m9; spelling 1–♭3–5–♭7–9).
Note	A single musical event having identifiable pitch.
Octave	An interval encompassing eight note names, for example, C–C. Two notes separated by a perfect octave (12 half steps) have the same name, are said to have the same pitch class, and are considered perfectly consonant.
Odd Time Signature	A time signature where the number of beats per measure is not a multiple of two or three. Examples: 5/8, 5/4, 7/8, 7/4, 11/8, 13/8.
Overtone Series	The sequence of frequencies in which each one is a whole multiple of a fundamental tone.
Outer Parts	The lowest and highest parts in a musical texture. In four-part harmony, the bass and soprano parts.
p	*Dynamic* marking: *piano* (soft).
Parallel Fifth	In four-part harmony and common practice in general, if two parts move in parallel motion and preserve an interval of a fifth or octave between them, this is known as a parallel fifth or octave (International English: *consecutive fifth/octave*), and is usually considered something to be avoided.
Parallel Motion	The phenomenon of two or more musical parts (particularly outer parts) moving in the same direction (ascending or descending) at the same time.
Parallel Octave	See *parallel fifth.*

Parallel Scale/Mode	A means of defining a scale or mode by comparison with another scale or mode on the same tonic note, as opposed to another scale broadly sharing the same set of notes (see *relative minor/major*). Most parallel comparisons tend to use the major scale as the reference point.
Part	1) The musical contribution of a single player within an ensemble and the notation representing this (as opposed to score). 2) A discreet horizontal strand associated with a pitch range within four-part harmony or derived discipline (see *SATB*).
Partials	A component of fundamental frequencies that comprise the *overtone series*.
Pause Mark	The symbol ⌢ , indicating that a note or chord is to be held for longer than its written value, interrupting the underlying pulse. Also called a *fermata*.
Pentatonic Scale	Any scale consisting of five notes per octave. In Western music, the most common pentatonic scales are the major pentatonic (1–2–3–5–6) and minor pentatonic (1–♭3–4–5–♭7). These share the same relative major/minor relationship as the major and natural minor scales. Major and minor pentatonics connected by this relationship share the same set of notes.
Percussion Stave	A loose notation system for percussion instruments where rhythms are written using one or more lines with each line or space usually represents a different instrument.
Perfect Cadence	A cadence consisting of the chord progression V–I. Also known as a "full close."
Perfect Interval	An interval that sounds among the most consonant intervals. Only fourths, fifths, and octaves (and their compound intervals) may be defined as perfect.
Phrygian Mode	The third mode of the major scale. In parallel terms, the Phrygian mode can be seen as a major scale with flatted second, third, sixth, and seventh steps.
Pitch	The distinction of "highness" versus "lowness" of musical notes. Closely connected to *frequency*.
Pitch Class	The group of notes sharing the same name, regardless of octave. For example, all Cs or all E♭s.
Plagal Cadence	A cadence consisting of the chord progression IV–I. Also known as an "amen cadence."
Polychord	A complex chord which can be analyzed as consisting of several simpler chords rather than using one longer chord symbol. A forward slash may be used to separate the chord names. If either chord is a major triad "maj" should be used to avoid implying a single note as in a slash chord. A horizontal separator may also be used. Examples: E♭m/Cmaj7; A7/Cm.
Polymeter	Describes music written using several time signatures concurrently.
Polyphony	Music with some rhythmic independence between parts, and usually some rhythmic and melodic interplay between them. (Adjective: polyphonic). Contrasts with *homophony*.
Polyrhythm	The occurrence of two or more different rhythmic divisions at once. For example, eighth note triplets at the same time as regular eighth notes. See also *cross-rhythm* and *hemiola*.

Polytonality	Describes music written in several keys at once, often a different key for each instrument or group of instruments. See also *bitonality*.
Power Chord	A chord type often used in rock music, having a root and fifth but no third. Power chords are thus neither major or minor and can be used in place of either. Also known as a 5 chord (A5, F#5, etc.)
Pulse	The underlying, regular rhythmic foundation in most music, consisting of the repetition of a beat (actual or implied) at regular time intervals.
Quarter Note	A note having a quarter of the duration of a whole note. Represents one beat in all time signatures where the lower number is 4 (e.g. 2/4, 3/4, 4/4).
Quaver	(International English) *eighth note*
rall.	Abbreviation of *rallentando* (getting gradually slower). Similar to rit., though generally interpreted as a more pronounced change.
Relative Major	See *relative minor*
Relative Minor	The relationship between a major key and the minor key sharing the same key signature whose tonic note is a minor third lower. For example, A minor is the relative minor of C major.
Resolution	The moment when a note causing dissonance within a chord or texture is replaced by a more consonant note. For example, when a suspended fourth resolves to the major third.
Rest	A symbol denoting a period of silence of a specified rhythmic value within a musical part.
rit.	Abbreviation of *ritardando* (getting gradually slower). Often used at the end of a piece. See also *rall*.
Roman Numeral Analysis	The system of musical analysis based on numbering scale steps (and the chords built on them) using Roman numerals.
Root	The note from which a chord is built (usually using thirds) and which gives it its name.
Root Position Chord	A chord with the root note in the bass, i.e., not an inversion.
SATB	Abbreviation of *soprano, alto, tenor, bass*. See *four-part harmony*.
Scale	An ascending/descending sequence of notes. In the major/minor key system, a scale draws on the notes of a key signature to define the sound of the key.
Score	The combination of the parts for all the players in a piece of music to represent the entire musical work, usually by means of multiple staves with one part/player on each stave, so that all musical events occurring simultaneously are aligned vertically.
Second (interval)	An interval encompassing two note names, for example, C–D. Commonly either major (two half steps), minor (one half step), or augmented (three half steps).
Second Inversion	A chord where the fifth is used as the bass note. For example, a C major chord with G in the bass.

Segno	Italian for "sign." A point in a piece marked to indicate a point to return to before playing either to a point marked *Fine* (end) or *To Coda*. See *D.S.*, *Coda*, *Fine* 𝄋
Semibreve	(International English) *whole note*
Semiquaver	(International English) *16th note*
Sequence	The statement and reiteration of melodic or harmonic material transposed to a higher or lower pitch.
Serialism	Atonal music written using sequences of all twelve notes in the octave, which may be stated and modified in various ways.
Seventh (interval)	An interval encompassing seven note names. For example, C–B. Commonly either major (eleven half steps), minor (ten half steps), or diminished (nine half steps).
Seventh Chord	A four-note chord which, when constructed in full, contains a root note, third, fifth, and seventh.
sfz	*Dynamic* marking: *sforzando* (with force).
Sharp	The ♯ symbol, placed to the left of a note as an accidental, or in the key signature, to indicate that a given note (which would otherwise be a natural) should be raised by a half step.
Simple Time	A meter or time signature where the basic pulse is divided by two rather than three using standard (rather than dotted) note values to represent beats and subdivisions. Examples: 2/4, 3/4, 4/4, 3/2.
Sine Wave	The simplest and purest possible waveform for any sound, consisting of a fundamental but no harmonics.
Sixteenth Note	A note having a 16th of the duration of a whole note. ♬
Sixth (interval)	An interval encompassing six note names. For example, C–A. Commonly either major (nine half steps), minor (eight half steps), or augmented (ten half steps).
Sixth Chord	A four-note chord containing a third, fifth, and sixth above the root note.
Slash Chord	A chord symbol where a bass note is specified after the main symbol, often used to indicate an inversion or as a means of avoiding a more complex chord name.
Soprano	The highest standardized human voice range, usually sung by female voices (child or adult) or male child voices. 2) The highest part in four-part harmony, usually carrying the melody.
Specific Interval	A fully defined interval described by the number of scale steps or letter names encompassed and further defined as perfect, major, minor, diminished, or augmented.
Stave/Staff	The arrangement of one or more lines (usually five) on which musical notes and/or rhythms are placed.
sub.	*Subito* (suddenly). Precedes a dynamic marking (usually *sub.* **pp** - suddenly quiet).

Suspension	A harmonic device whereby one or more notes in a chord are substituted for others that seem to want to resolve to the note replaced, whether or not this actually happens. For example, the suspended fourth chord (symbol: sus4) contains a perfect fourth from the root instead of a third, which may be resolved down to the third.
Swing	A rhythmic characteristic particularly associated with jazz, whereby eighth (or sometimes 16th) notes are not evenly spaced; the offbeats are placed late, arriving closer to the following beat. At slow-to-medium tempos, the relationship is essentially the same as the quarter/eight combination in compound time; at faster tempos, the lengths tend to be a little closer to equal.
Tablature	A notation system which uses numbers to represent the frets of an instrument such as a guitar on a stave where each string is represented by its own line.
Temperament	Any tuning system devised to compensate for the disadvantages of pythagorean tuning so that more keys will be useable. The logical conclusion of this is equal temperament. Other temperaments are rarely used in modern music.
Tempo	The speed of the musical pulse, specified using either words or numbers (beats per minute).
Tenor	1) The second-lowest standardized human voice range, usually sung by male voices. 2) The second-lowest part in four-part harmony, and thus one of the inner parts.
Tenor Clef	A clef most often used to notate the upper notes of instruments that otherwise use the bass clef, such as the cello. On a five-line stave, the tenor clef defines the second line down as middle C.
Third (interval)	An interval encompassing three note names. For example, C–E. Commonly either major (four half steps) or minor (three half steps).
Third Inversion	A chord where the seventh is used as the bass note, for example a C7 chord with B♭ in the bass.
Thirteenth Chord	A chord which may contain a third, fifth, seventh, ninth, 11th, and 13th from the root note. The dominant 13th (symbol: 13; spelling: 1–3–5–♭7–9–(11)–13) usually omits the 11th and often also the fifth and/or ninth.
Thirty-Second Note	A note having a 32nd of the duration of a whole note.
Tierce de Picardie	The use of the tonic major chord as the final chord in a piece or movement in a minor key. For example, an A major chord ending a piece in A minor. Also known in English as a "Picardy Third."
Time Signature	The indication usually comprising two numbers (upper and lower) defining the number of beats in a measure and the note value used to represent each beat (lower number).
Tonality	The character of a piece of music as a function of the type of scale or mode defined by its key. Examples include major, minor, and the various modes.

Tonic	The note giving its name to a musical key and felt to be the musical center or "home" note in that key.
Transposing Instrument	An instrument whose notes are transposed by a fixed interval relative to most (non-transposing) instruments.
Treble Clef	The most common clef in use, particularly for melody instruments. On a five-line stave, the treble clef defines the second line up as the note G above middle C.
Triad	A three-note chord, usually consisting of a root, third, and fifth.
Triple Time	A time signature in which three primary pulses are felt.
12-Bar Blues	A chord sequence central to the development of blues, jazz, and rock music. Its original form used only chords I, IV, and V, usually all as dominant sevenths. Modified versions using more advanced harmony are found particularly in jazz.
Waltz	A European dance, usually felt in 3/4 time.
Whole Note	The note value in modern music notation from which all other note values (half, quarter, etc.) are defined. 𝗼

ABOUT THE AUTHOR

Tom Fleming is a guitarist, producer, arranger, and author, and he has enjoyed a highly varied career since graduating from Leeds College of Music with a degree in Jazz Studies. He is active across a wide range of musical styles from jazz and rock to musical theatre, and he has played a role in the creation of major educational resources, including Trinity College London's Rock & Pop grade exam syllabus.

www.tomflemingmusic.co.uk